personal
paths
to Humanism

Personal
Paths
to Humanism

HUMANIST PRESS

WASHINGTON DC

Printed book ISBN: 978-0-931779-71-8
Ebook ISBN: 978-0-931779-69-5

66 I will not follow
where the path
may lead, but I
will go where
there is no path,
and I will
leave a trail."

–Muriel Strode

Contents

Introduction...1

Brant Abrahamson..............................6

Debbie Allen 11

Emma Bates....................................18

Helen Bennett 22

Bob Bhaerman 28

Rob Boston....................................33

Lori Lipman Brown..............................37

Lucille Cormier 43

Fred Edwords 48

Rebecca Newberger Goldstein 54

Han Hills 60

Sikivu Hutchinson...............................65

Arthur Jackson 69

Margaret Placentra Johnston....................74

Marissa Torres Langseth 79

Nancy Martin...................................84

Raúl Martínez 88

James Nguyen 93

Vivek Palavali 100

Steven Pinker 106

Anthony Pinn..................................110

Harold Saferstein 115

Herb Silverman................................118

Sharon Stanley................................123

Todd Stiefel...................................129

Derrick Strobl 134

Carol Wintermute 140

Introduction

Humanism is more than a body of great ideas. It is people —human beings like you who make up a movement. And these people all have journeys and life stories. Since humanism so often functions as an alternative to the traditional religious ideas with which many were raised, those journeys can include realizations and struggles that led these individuals to abandon one set of answers and adopt another.

Perhaps you have a story of how you came to humanism. There may have been a particular path you took. And you might think that your experience is unique. Or maybe you think it is just like everyone else's. But is it?

What does it feel like to come to humanism from Catholicism, Protestantism, Judaism, Hinduism, or even a secular outlook? What if the religion of one's childhood was mild, or strict? Can people leave traditional faith at an early age or does it always take a long time? And can the change come suddenly and all at once or must it always involve study and a gradual personal evolution?

For scientist and 2006 Humanist of the Year Steven Pinker it came in two ways:

One was a gradual development in my professional life as a cognitive scientist. My conviction that the mind is a product of the brain, that the brain is a product of evolution, and that moral systems must be informed by a scientific mindset, led me to question the common belief that religion is a major source of morality. The other was sudden: coming across the many passages from the Old Testament in which God commands his people to commit rape and genocide.

The variety in such transformations, and their causes, can be stunning. But so can the similarities. When we listen to others tell how they found their way to our own worldview, both the familiar and unfamiliar in their experiences can bind us to them, create a kinship between us. We not only learn but we identify.

And we come to realize that humanist ideas aren't only a set of philosophical abstractions. They are living things, they are arrived at by processes of change, and therefore they are personally transforming. Grasping this puts the *human* in humanism. And because humans are social animals who bond over shared experiences, this makes humanist *community* possible. So the power of humanist ideas extends from the philosophical to the psychological to the sociological. And that helps explain the explosion of local and national humanist groups around the world that are bringing humanists together in various ways. The ideas are in the air, the personal changes are unfolding, and the humanist communities are thriving.

It should be felt as no surprise then that, as our humanist movement grows, we hear more and more personal stories. For example, readers of the January/February 2016 issue of the *Humanist* magazine (the seventy-fifth anniversary issue) are treated to three articles on the theme "In Their Own Words: Humanists Discuss Their Paths to Humanism."

The 1993 Humanist Heroine, Barbara G. Walker, writes about her "conversion" as a young girl who, after an effort to communicate with and confront God, "came to the conclusion that I spoke into a celestial telephone with no one on the other end. All those fears had been put into me for nothing. He wasn't there at all!" So she decided, "Never again would I be mentally or emotionally enslaved by a cruel mythology."

T. Hamish Tear writes movingly about the joint passing of his parents, whose lives the family celebrated with a humanist funeral in Scotland, and how the inspiring nature of that service brought him to humanism. Today, after having discovered the American Humanist Association, he writes, "I am in fascinated study of the philosophies of the AHA and numerous other secular groups. This learning shapes the ways in which I now see and think about people, societies, and world order. It gives me insight into forming the mission of a new AHA chapter in Wyoming."

Jason Holden became a humanist when in a federal prison and, seeking an alternative to his institution's support of religious programming, won the right to form humanist study groups there where prisoners can develop positive narratives through humanist ethics.

To collect such experiences and the life histories of AHA members—and preserve them in a perpetual archive for the benefit of future generations—the late Bette Chambers, AHA president from 1973 to 1979, created the Humanist Heritage Program. Her goal was to build an institutional history of the American Humanist Association and the humanist movement.

Today that work has been accelerated through the sponsorship of the Humanist Foundation, the AHA's endowment fund. Under that leadership, arrangements are now in progress for an archivist to catalog the mass of material collected so far and make it available not only for the organization's own use but for qualified researchers. Over the years there have been frequent requests by advanced-degree candidates and journalists who have been granted access to the files of the organization's early pioneers and leaders.

And routinely today, new material is actively solicited by the Humanist Foundation from all humanists who have remembered the AHA or the Foundation in their will or other estate plan. Participants are thus encouraged to leave more than a monetary legacy but a personal one as well—indicating their place and date of birth, describing their early family years, revealing the religion or philosophy of their parents, naming schools attended and degrees earned, and chronicling their professional as well as personal lives. But perhaps most importantly, participants are asked about their humanism: how they define it, how it has influenced their lives, and to what extent it has been expressed in work with humanist and allied organizations. Finally, participants are invited to give their assessment of the greater humanist movement: its goals, directions, and future.

In the spirit of all this, with the aim of letting the effort become more widely known and the stories more widely told, a project was launched to produce a small book that would "explore how a number of our members set out on their individual and unique paths to humanism." Toward that end, a somewhat random selection of humanist activists was asked to respond to a prepared set of questions about their journeys and how humanism influenced their daily and professional lives. That set of questions was as follows:

1. What set you on your path to humanism?

2. What religious traditions, if any, did you leave behind?

3. What "pot holes" did you see in the traditions of your previous religious experiences?

4. Did you have a "Road to Damascus" experience where you suddenly became a humanist or was your experience more transitional?

5. How did your family, friends, and colleagues react when you told them about your path to humanism?

6. What suggestions would you give others who now follow a path to humanism?

7. Did you find that your position impacted others to consider making a similar move as yours?

8. What does being a humanist mean to you?

9. What distinguishes humanism from other ways of thinking?

10. How did you find the American Humanist Association and how do you feel it promotes your convictions?

Now we have their responses, collected together in this little volume. And so impressed are we by the nature of their narratives that we have decided to call this "Volume 1" and prepare ourselves to receive more personal stories for the next volume. If you wish to provide your own biography for inclusion in the AHA archives or for consideration as a submission to the next volume of *Personal Paths to Humanism*, we will gratefully receive it (preferably, in the form of a Microsoft Word file) at:

Humanist Heritage Program
1777 T Street NW | Washington, DC 20009
Heritage@AmericanHumanist.org

Meanwhile, we hope the descriptions of the roads traveled by this first group of contributors will resonate with you. And for those non-humanists who encounter this collection, we hope these stories will broaden your understanding of how and why people become humanists. For it is such experiences that reveal who we are, what we want, and where we intend to go in the world.

—Bob Bhaerman and Fred Edwords

Brant **Abrahamson**

Brant Abrahamson, now eighty, has long distributed humanistic lesson materials to high school students through Teachers Pay Teachers, The Teachers' Press, and the American Humanist Association. These lessons were developed out of his thirty-two years of high school teaching. Being selected as an Illinois Master Teacher inspired him to continue making these lessons available to other educators after his retirement.

❡❡

was born during the Great Depression and reared on a farm, growing up in the liberal Evangelical Lutheran tradition. On most weeks my siblings and I went to Sunday school, after which the whole family would sit together during the hour-long congregational service. At Christmastime I would participate in the Christmas pageant and in summer go to Bible school. Later, in junior high, I attended the church's Saturday morning confirmation class and, in high school, actively participated in the Luther League organization and went to a Lutheran summer Bible camp.

My family ate meals together that always began with a short prayer, and we said prayers at bedtime as well. But religion didn't "hang heavy in the air" in our household. In fact, my family and community might be considered "humanist" in that moral instruction focused on being fair, helping others, doing one's share of work, keeping emotions under control, being reliable, and not wasting resources. Rewards and punishments were small and earthly.

Despite some teenage failings, I came to be admired for being a good Christian. Some church members even thought I would become a minister. But aspects of Christianity troubled me from an early age. The Adam and Eve story seemed improbable, as did the Resurrection. Being a farm boy, I'd seen many dead animals and couldn't imagine how anything dead for three days could come back to life. When I asked about God's vengeful acts, my mother said, "Well, that's just the Old Testament." About the gore in Revelation? "It's difficult to understand." Although creationism was taught in Sunday school, my parents accepted evolutionary principles, saying, "This is how God did it."

Nonetheless, I seriously considered the ministry when in 1954 I arrived at Augustana College, our church school and seminary in Rock Island, Illinois. College leaders tried to keep us within the faith, and we had to attend chapel and take a course on Christianity. So I probably told myself that, as a clergyman, I could help people live better lives and get to heaven. But as I look back, I can see that I was doing little more than playing the role expected of me. Therefore, without any deep feeling of commitment, I let the idea of becoming a member of the clergy fade. And Christianity itself ceased to be of central importance for me when earthly concerns took center stage. I married before I graduated in 1959.

From 1959 to 1961, I studied political science at the University of Iowa, earning a Master of Arts degree. Then I began teaching social studies at Riverside Brookfield High School in Illinois, where I spent the next thirty-two years. My colleagues and I were given the responsibility of constructing a series of Global Area Studies. Since religious belief has been a driving force in most societies throughout history, we included a focus on religion. Our students learned about the world's dominant faiths from the perspective of an educated believer within each tradition. In addition, they learned about the wars and mass killings that religious beliefs sometimes fostered. As it happened, teaching this curriculum proceeded to drain from me any remaining identification with Christianity. But I still went to church, doing so for professional, social, and family reasons.

When I found myself divorced with two small children to bring up as a single parent, I decided for the sake of their moral education to continue with the Episcopalian church that my wife had brought us into. As a result, it wasn't until after they had grown and left home that I begin pursuing my own religious way.

My second wife, Grace, had been a Roman Catholic before we met but became alienated with that faith and was therefore willing to join me in attending the humanist-oriented Unitarian Universalist Church in Oak Park. This church provided a comfortable, traditional structure that was refreshingly without supernaturalism.

Later, however, when that church became more Christian-like, we switched to the Unitarian Church of Hinsdale, a humanistic congregation wherein an American Humanist Association chapter had formed. We thus came to learn more of the humanist philosophy. And after Hurricane Katrina in 2005, I went with a group of humanists to Mississippi to help rebuild.

I was widowed in 2011, after which I met my third wife, Nancy, at the Hinsdale church. We were married there in 2012, creating our own humanist ceremony. Howard Katz was our humanist celebrant.

Nancy's humanism differs somewhat from mine. She views herself as an existential humanist whereas, generally speaking, I approach humanism from historical and scientific perspectives. I'm very concerned with maintaining the separation of church and state and keeping creationism out of public schools. Her viewpoint is more empathetic in that she is deeply concerned about how people live now and how the quality of their lives can be improved. She has greatly increased my awareness of the many social issues with which humanists should be concerned.

My path to humanism has been gradual, winding, and is still evolving. As for my family, I have cousins who are creationists, an atheist brother who for fifty years has been married to a church-going Southern Baptist, and a sister who identifies with a form of

Gnostic Christianity. We accept the choices that family members have made and don't think it our business to pry into their beliefs. Moreover, most of us have humanistic ideas about how life should be lived. And many adults with whom I've associated have had views similar to mine, regardless of the labels they used.

Did this humane form of humanism affect my students over the years? I believe it did. I worked to broaden their perspectives, which often led them to more humanistic approaches to life. To the degree that I was admired as a teacher and as a parent, I may have influenced them toward this point of view. People tend to emulate those they look up to.

In addition, the instructional guidebooks that my colleague and I had written are still being requested and widely used. I recently mailed two units to the leader of a humanist group in the Iowa State Penitentiary.

This all leads me to recommend that, when it comes to rearing children, parents should teach by example and have open dialogue. They can also enroll their children in library and museum activities, a primary source of humanistic programs for children. And they should teach them about evolution. I further suggest that youngsters be enrolled in Unitarian Universalist Sunday school programs. Those with which I am familiar are thoroughly humanist. Indeed, I think that UU congregations—and liberal churches in general—are often halfway houses on the pathway to a full-fledged humanism.

❖

Debbie **Allen**

Debbie Allen is immediate past president of the Humanist Fellowship of San Diego, coordinator of the San Diego Coalition of Reason, board member of the American Humanist Association, board member of the Humanist Society, board member of the Reason Rally Coalition, Inc., and a volunteer humanist chaplain with the Humanist Society and the Military Association of Atheists and Freethinkers.

⑊

was born into a patchwork of Christian religions: primarily
Catholicism, Lutheranism, and Mormonism. My baptism was
Catholic, which was probably convenient for everyone since
my mother's mother was raised in that tradition. My mother
and father included prayers in our bedtime ritual, and we said
grace before important meals like Thanksgiving dinner. I was giv-
en the Christian understanding of God, Jesus, heaven and hell,
and the belief that being good might lead to everlasting life.

Not long before I was born, my mother's father converted to
Mormonism prior to marrying his second wife. My step-grand-
mother was a "true-believing Mormon" from Utah. Being only
slightly older than my parents, with no children of her own, she
enjoyed taking me to Primary meetings on Sunday mornings. My
parents probably encouraged this in order to have Sunday mornings to themselves, since they weren't churchgoers. For my part I
enjoyed Sunday school and have always had a fondness for, and
curiosity about, Mormons. I recall our family being visited several
times by young Mormon missionaries, arriving by bike and wear-
ing short-sleeved white shirts and ties. I was old enough to understand that my father wasn't going to quit smoking and my mother
wasn't going to give up coffee. Overall, however, I'm not sure what
they made of the doctrines and covenants of the Latter Day Saints,
since my family never discussed religion to any great extent.

But when I was about nine, they decided to try returning to a Lutheran congregation—my dad's boyhood faith—perhaps as a way to end the Mormon proselytizing and family concerns that they weren't providing their children with a proper religious education. So my brother and I were baptized Lutheran, and I was thrilled that the occasion called for a new dress, hat, and shoes. I immediately became involved in the youth choir, enjoyed Sunday school, and excelled at memorizing Bible verses. My parents soon tired of the Sunday morning commitment, but I kept going for the singing, the youth music performances, and the social activities.

There was only one problem for me amid all this. I was quite inquisitive, annoyingly assertive in expressing my own thoughts and opinions, and eager to challenge authority. From a young age I suspected that God did not exist and questioned religious "truth." Lying in bed at night I would wonder, "If God created the world, who created God?" We all know where this reasoning leads, and it made my very young head spin. Thus my path to humanism began with a perhaps innate skepticism and continued with a rejection of the worldview I had been assigned at birth.

It's no surprise, then, that my favorite "religious traditions" were entirely secular. My mother owned a seasonal Christmas store filled with elaborate handmade decorations. Not only did I make items to sell but I worked at the register every Saturday. I knew we were celebrating Jesus's birthday, but there was only a polite nod to this fact at our house and a complete indulgence in the pagan and secular traditions of Christmas. Every Easter I ate pounds of jelly beans, which we purchased to fill our homemade Easter gifts. I like to say that, in practice, we worshipped the holy trinity: Santa Claus, the Easter Bunny, and the Tooth Fairy.

It was during junior high school that I first called myself an atheist. I'm sure it had to do with my doubt about mythological characters being real and my growing interest in science and human nature. When I was in the eighth grade I announced my atheism to my family while out to dinner one evening. There was a slight pause in the conversation and someone said, "No you're not," like I was too young to make such a pronouncement. But I never became a believer.

When I was in high school my best girlfriend and the boy I thought I'd marry were both born-again Christians. In my characteristic style of supporting the passions of others and having a willingness to stretch my own boundaries, I read the *Good News Bible* (the hip translation of the New Testament published in the 1970s) and attended meetings of Young Life (a Christian youth organization). But I remained, quite proudly, an atheist. Religion wasn't important in my family life, nor was it the glue that connected the members of my extended family. The Catholics, the Protestants, the Mormons, and the deists all got along. I was active in student government, sports, and various music performance groups and took little notice of the religious lives of my friends and neighbors.

I was, however, unwilling to have anyone pray at my high school graduation. So, as the student body officer in charge of planning the event, I assigned myself the role of delivering the invocation. I made certain that it was entirely secular (with no praying to anyone). It's ironic that the very next day I was playing "Pomp and Circumstance" on the piano as my graduating class celebrated during some kind of school-sponsored service at a local Methodist church.

Because I was an atheist at such a young age, I don't think I was sufficiently aware of the philosophical issues with any particular religion or denomination. Rather, I think I noticed that the people I loved, admired, and respected were headed in different directions on Sunday mornings, or sleeping in. To me, religious preferences had more to do with style than substance, since I was fully convinced that God did not exist—for any of them.

It was not insignificant, however, that I was aware of the different treatment of men and of women, and especially of men of color, in the Mormon church. I was concerned with civil rights issues in high school and was focused on equality for minorities and women. My fascination with culture also led to reading other religious texts as well as books critical of mainstream religions.

As my world grew, so did my awareness of various worldviews and the understanding that people throughout the ages created gods and goddesses, and worshipped them because they "believed." Their insistence on having the "truth" was the same as that of my believing relatives.

Hence my path to humanism was entirely transitional. I became an atheist interested in studying anthropology, psychology, and cognitive development with the goal of being a teacher or a psychologist. And my worldview was expanded exponentially in college when I started studying the family systems and mores of other cultures. What I thought of as "normal" in southern California was anything but the norm.

During my graduate studies, I was exposed to great philosophers and cultural critics and was especially fond of the existentialists—although that period did exacerbate my own existential crisis. I admired their struggle to grasp the nature of reality and search for meaning in their lives. As a young psychotherapist, I was trained to set aside my own biases—a process which assumes you are struggling to determine what those are. While this allowed me to effectively work within the philosophical framework of my clients to facilitate healing, it also made me increasingly frustrated with the often nonsensical, and sometimes detrimental, adherence to religious dogma.

After a period of searching for an alternative to the religious nonsense espoused by adult friends and acquaintances, as well as a desire to be part of a community committed to social justice, I converted to Judaism in my thirties within a liberal Reform congregation. I did so as an atheist and was warmly welcomed by my progressive rabbis. Fellow congregants weren't interested in what I believed but instead focused on what I was *doing* to "repair the world" *(tikkun olam)*. I immediately became involved in chairing various committees, including Outreach to Interfaith, Social Action, Adult Education, and Membership. I also for six years served on the board of directors of this 1,300-family synagogue. My extended family and closest friends attended my ceremonial conversion to Judaism as well as my adult bat mitzvah and a few traditional holiday celebrations. The people who were most interested in the path I was on were my liberal religious and "spiritual" friends. They understood and respected the joy and benefits of affiliating with a community that was personally enriching and intellectually challenging.

It was during a conference of the Union for Reform Judaism that I stumbled on an Americans United for Separation of Church and State table in the exhibition area. This was the beginning of a more focused education in secular values and my eventual association with secular organizations. Through active participation in the latter, I have met hundreds of people and enjoyed happy and rewarding experiences full of new challenges and opportunities.

Since then friends, family, neighbors, acquaintances, and even strangers have weighed in. Some agree with me and are encouraging; others are not. I was initially surprised that more people didn't join me in my participation in humanist organizations, conferences, and causes. Most are comfortable in their own lifestyle and are well established in their social and cultural communities.

So no fantastic deconversions have resulted nor have many joined the American Humanist Association or the Humanist Fellowship of San Diego (the humanist chapter of which I was president). I was, however, able to entice my brother's family to attend an AHA conference held near their home in 2009, and I sent my nieces to Camp Quest the following two summers.

As for the family members and friends who thought I was a heathen and doomed to hell, they were largely silent (i.e., praying for me on Sundays) but fond of saying, "We love you anyway." I don't think they realize how insulting that sounds.

What suggestions would I give others who now follow a path to humanism? Allow yourself great enthusiasm for your process of discovery. Challenging old ideas, as well as evaluating new ones, requires open-mindedness and courage. You must also be prepared to accept that new knowledge and experiences may alter your course yet again. Do not diminish your joy by trying to convince others that you are right. Plenty of people will agree with you, but there are a limited number who truly love you and value you in precisely the way that most families and friends are capable of.

It is difficult to part ways with old friends, but my new friends are kind, loving, intellectually challenging, and always interesting. My life is richer for sharing what matters to me with others who have a similar worldview. And when I give my time, energy, and contributions to help my local humanist community as well as the national American Humanist Association, I feel confident that I am contributing to creating a better world.

❖

Emma **Bates**

Emma Bates is an actress and humanist living and working in Los Angeles. Currently she is involved in outreach efforts on behalf of the American Humanist Association and the Foundation Beyond Belief. She has also done extensive consulting, outreach, and viral video production for the Richard Dawkins Foundation and is a fellow of the Humanist Community Project at Harvard.

I always have had a big imagination. As a child, if there was a rainbow, I was off running to find the pot of gold at the end of it. I believed in Santa Claus, in guardian angels, and that piranhas lived under my bed at night. Learning to distinguish reality from imagination is the work of adolescence. But magical thinking is humanity's default mode, and overcoming this impulse is a continual process. I have learned along the way that many adults don't ever fully cross this bridge. On the other side of this bridge for me was humanism.

I was raised culturally Christian, but we were never frequent churchgoers. In any case, my parents liked to cherry-pick different aspects from all the religions. I think they were more interested in the community aspect of church than in the doctrine. My grandmother converted to Judaism when I was a child, so I was exposed to that as well. Mostly, we were taught to treat people with kindness and to "do unto others as you would have them do to you."

Overall, I was raised to believe in God as a protector and benevolent force. So in early adulthood, without much examination, I continued to see this to be generally true. In fact, by that time I carried with me such an amalgam of religious viewpoints that contradictions among them weren't immediately obvious to me. I had made God anything I needed him to be, so I'd just adjust around any difficulties that came up. And since I didn't subscribe to any particular dogma, I merely considered myself spiritual. It was a huge blind spot for me.

In my late twenties, I decided it was time to really form an opinion about religion and get my questions answered. So for about nine months I studied all the major religions intensely and critically. By the end of my study, I was an atheist. I had also learned to think critically and deeply in a way that I never had before. I did this by being patient and allowing myself to be comfortable with cognitive dissonance.

I haven't experienced a lot of backlash from my family. Some have even come to the same conclusion over time. My friends are primarily made up of other artists and tend to be freethinkers by nature. Not many of them are interested in religion, or humanism for that matter. My experience is that a lot of artists find meaning primarily through their work.

There is a part in the Chekhov play *Three Sisters* that I love where Masha is lamenting that she and her sisters know five languages, can play musical instruments, and are educated but they are of no use in the provincial little town they live in. The character Vershinin goes into a monologue about how being even one person in that town who is educated matters, and how it affects everyone with whom they come in contact. He says that because of her and her sisters "in two hundred years life will be unimaginably beautiful" in that town. I've always liked that scene because it touches on something I do believe in. I do think it matters what you think and that it does have impact on the people with whom you come into contact. How you think and what you believe changes your behavior. I see this translated politically all the time. These small shifts have seismic effects over time.

So if there is any advice I would give to others who are on a path that leads them to humanism, it would be for them to get involved in nonreligious activist communities. There is so much discrimination in the name of religion that needs to be rectified, and we need all the help we can get. I would also suggest they be open about their views if they are in a safe position to do so.

To sum everything up, to me being a humanist means being kind and being a truth seeker. It is what I felt like I have always been doing naturally. Part of my finding truth has been rejecting all the supernatural answers. I believe that humanism promotes critical thinking, a skill that must be learned and honed throughout life.

I began working with the American Humanist Association after having worked with the Richard Dawkins Foundation and the Humanist Community at Harvard. I started by creating and directing the viral video of Richard reading his hate mail. I think it is fun and necessary to add a little humor into this movement when possible. I make video content and help coordinate celebrity outreach to try and raise the public profile of humanism. And I believe the AHA does a great job at being at the forefront of the political action that is so necessary for humanism in America. The organization has both a strong national and local presence that is vital to getting anything accomplished. It also creates room for dialogue and community building, two things that will have ripple effects for many years to come.

❖

Helen **Bennett**

Helen Bennett, an author and poet, is a former high school and university English teacher, university and children's librarian, and editor. She is now a volunteer teacher of adults at the Unitarian Universalist Friendship Fellowship at Pineda, Florida, and at SAIL (Senior Adventures in Learning) in Melbourne, Florida. She has degrees from Brooklyn College, the University of Wisconsin at Madison, the University of California at Berkeley, and Florida Atlantic University.

I came to humanism largely through reading and then through the humanist group I joined when I first became a Unitarian Universalist. As a young student studying at Brooklyn College, I encountered the writings of Bertrand Russell in my philosophy classes. Having used his *History of Western Philosophy* as a textbook, I also read his essays "Why I Am Not a Christian" and "What Is an Agnostic?" These were revelatory to me! I didn't know that a Christian could renounce his religion and reveal his agnosticism so rationally. It made sense to me, and I immediately became an agnostic. It took many more decades before I became a full-fledged humanist, as I was not aware of that lifestance until 1995.

I was raised in Brooklyn as an only child in a largely secular Jewish family. We celebrated the Passover Seder with my grandparents, and that was a highlight of the year. The High Holidays were the only times my parents went to the synagogue and my mother said *yiskor*, the prayer for the dead. On Yom Kippur we walked five subway stations to the home of my aunt and uncle where we broke our fast. I continued to fast on Yom Kippur until well into adulthood.

I learned a few Yiddish words from my parents and came to enjoy Jewish foods such as gefilte fish, chopped liver, and matzo. For some reason my children never acquired these tastes! Although both of my sons had Orthodox bar mitzvahs, they married

Christian women and drifted away from Judaism. They do observe Jewish holidays in a cursory way, however. (The only reason for the Orthodox bar mitzvahs was that my sons were taught privately by an Orthodox rabbi. We ourselves were mostly non-observant Conservative Jews who could never find a temple or synagogue that we liked. My husband said the prayers at home but I did not.)

When my older son Michael was planning to get married, I visited the Unitarian Universalist Church of Fort Lauderdale. There I discovered a pamphlet about the positive advantages of interfaith marriage. I was delighted, but Michael and his bride were not interested in a UU ceremony or in that religion. A few years later my husband died, and I hastened over to the UU Church where a dear friend was a member. I joined one month later after a serious talk with the minister, who assured me that Jesus was not worshipped there.

The humanist group in Fort Lauderdale was a "godsend" to me. I loved that group and rejoiced in finding my unique niche at last. My poem "Prayer" became a big hit with the group, as it imagined God himself telling me that he did not exist but was just a "figment" of my imagination. It ended with God saying,

I can't affect your family, your fortune or your health
In truth, I cannot help you
You can only help yourself.

This poem, and its two sequels, became the basis of my "Conversation with God: Humanism vs. Theism," which was presented, along with three other such Conversations, at different Unitarian Universalist congregations. In all these dialogues, God assured me of his non-existence.

While I had heard the name, it wasn't until 1999 I finally discovered who Robert Ingersoll was. Many articles appeared in the humanist literature on the centenary of his death. He became my biggest hero, and I read many of his books and sayings. I taught about Ingersoll whenever and wherever I could, as I believe that the nineteenth century "Great Agnostic" was way ahead of his time—and ours. I developed a program in which I had a dialogue with Ingersoll and presented it in two different Unitarian Universalist congregations. I was thrilled when an elderly UU friend, Tony Rosamilia, bequeathed to me his most prized possession: the complete Dresden edition of Ingersoll's works, from 1900, in twelve volumes.

I have read humanist and atheist authors such as Richard Dawkins, Mason Olds, Christopher Hitchens, Jennifer Michael Hecht, Corliss Lamont, Sam Harris, Michael Parenti, Greg Epstein, Carl Sagan, Daniel Dennett, Paul Kurtz, Mark Twain (*Letters from the Earth* and *The Bible According to Mark Twain*), Steve Allen, Rebecca Goldstein, and Susan Jacoby. The latter inspired me with her books *Freethinkers*, *The Age of American Unreason*, *The Great Agnostic*, and *Half-Jew*. (Humanist Jacoby found out she was half Jewish only when she was a young adult, as her father had hidden that "shameful" fact from her.)

One of the most influential factors in my humanism was the book of sermons by John H. Dietrich, *What if the World Went Humanist?* Dietrich was one of the first Unitarians (with Curtis W. Reese) to break with theism early in the twentieth century. I used his sermon, "What Is a Liberal?" in one of my UU presentations. Dietrich knew that the world would *not* go humanist but said if it did, "There would be immediate recognition of the essential unity of mankind ... that there flows through the whole human race ... one life and one blood, that we have a common life and interest. ... This would mean the elimination of all racial antagonisms, national jealousies, class struggles, religious prejudices, and individual hatreds." Dietrich also said, "The real humanist experiences a kind of mystical ecstasy that comes from the conviction of humanity's dependence upon itself."

Such forward-looking Unitarians and others formulated the *first* Humanist Manifesto, with its socialist leanings, in 1933. There followed a *more detailed* Humanist Manifesto in 1973 and a *more succinct one* in 2003, which I happily signed. I have never deviated from my devotion to the humanist philosophy, though I consider myself a religious rather than a secular humanist. Both kinds are nontheistic, but a religious humanist belongs to a congregation, such as in Unitarian Universalism, Humanistic Judaism, or Ethical Culture, and is more community-oriented than individualist.

My closest relatives, my sons Michael and Danny, have not objected to my new philosophy of humanism. My children's book, *Humanism, What's That? A Book for Curious Kids*, which was published in 2005, has provided me with wonderful feedback. I was thrilled to find out that it recently was distributed by freethinkers in public schools in Kentucky as a rejoinder to the distribution of New Testaments. It is ironic that my little book starts out with a fierce proclamation of the primacy of separation of church and state! I know my stance has influenced some adults to become humanists, since a brilliant college student of mine who edited my book before it was published told me so. Also, a highly educated man told me that my book revealed his innate humanism to him—and he joined my humanist group!

I joined the American Humanist Association when I first became a humanist in the mid-1990s, and for several years I was president of the AHA chapter, the Humanists of Brevard, in

Central Florida. When a delegate from the AHA visited our Fellowship and started a chapter there, I was named president by acclamation. I am glad that my congregation at Friendship Fellowship at Pineda is mostly humanist, and I have delivered several humanistic sermons there. I am proud to be a humanist as it is the lifestance that provides the simplest and best explanation of our purpose here on earth—and even prouder to be a humanist author, in the company of the great authors I listed above as my mentors.

❖

Bob **Bhaerman**

Bob Bhaerman, EdD, from Pickerington, Ohio—a suburb of Columbus—serves as an educational consultant to the American Humanist Association. The focus of his most recent research and writing is on secular humanism in literature. He has taught at all levels—elementary school and college—and has been a secular humanist since his undergraduate days.

I was born in Brooklyn, New York, in 1932 during the Great Depression. My father lost his job as a clothing worker a few weeks after I was born. Outside of a few jobs in the Works Progress Administration, he was unemployed until 1938. Then he found work in a pants factory and we moved to a small town in northeastern Pennsylvania, Forty Fort. This was mainly a Protestant town of about 3,500 people. There were only about six or eight Jewish families, of which we were one.

I say that we were Jewish, but this was in name only. My father went to a synagogue only on Yom Kippur, and then not every year, and my mother didn't keep kosher (although she never served pork products or shellfish). Religion was little recognized in our house. I never had a bar mitzvah and never received any Hanukkah gelt. People have asked me if I was Orthodox, Conservative, Reform, or Reconstructionist. My response: "I was vacuum packed."

When I was a freshman in college majoring in education, a friend of mine gave me a pamphlet about the religious education of children. It was written by Algernon D. Black, a leader in the New York Society for Ethical Culture. The pamphlet really registered with me, so the next time I was New York City I attended the Sunday morning platform there. It happened that the speaker was Dr. Black himself. Although I can't remember what he spoke about that morning, whatever he said really hit home. I recall the feeling I had that day, that I had found a home.

I graduated from Wilkes College (now Wilkes University), then received a master's degree from Pennsylvania State University and a Doctor of Education from Rutgers University. After graduating from Penn State I taught fifth grade in Bloomfield, New Jersey, and later taught education courses at Wilkes, Hunter College in the Bronx (now Lehman College), the University of Delaware, and the State University College in Oneonta, New York.

Later I had a series of research positions in several organizations: the American Federation of Teachers (where I was also director of the education issues department), the Center for Research in Vocational Education at Ohio State University, Research for Better Schools (the education laboratory in Philadelphia), and the Corporation for National and Community Service (where I was coordinator of school-based service learning in Learn and Serve America). In these positions, I wrote a variety of publications on issues relating to school-to-work, career education, service-learning, and other educational issues. I also served for a time as associate dean of research and graduate studies in the College of Education at Wayne State University.

When I was a teacher I was also a member of various Ethical Culture societies. In Bloomfield I was a member of the Essex County society and, when I taught at Hunter, was a member of the New York society. More recently, I was one of the organizers of the American Ethical Union's Ethical Society without Walls, the group that serves people who don't live near an Ethical Culture congregation.

I married Jane Doran, a Roman Catholic. We were married by a former leader of the Ethical Humanist Society of Philadelphia. Needless to say, a number of her relatives didn't attend our wedding, declaring: "Ethical Culture, what the hell is that?"

We had four children, one of whom, Douglas, was born with a severe birth defect and died in four days. David is now fifty-two and Dan is forty-two. Robin, who sadly suffered from depression and bipolar disorder, took her own life at age forty-four.

Jane, who wanted our children to have some kind of religious education, decided to enroll them in the Sunday school at a Reform temple in Alexandria, Virginia, and later in Columbus, Ohio, where they had bar and bat mitzvahs. None of them followed through with their Jewish education. Jane didn't encourage it and neither did I. In fact, Jane became involved in a Unitarian Universalist church in Columbus and was active in it until her death in 2006. For my part, I enjoyed hearing the talks and, especially, attending the social functions. I am now a member of the American Humanist Association's chapter, the Humanist Community of Central Ohio.

In August 2010 I graduated from the Humanist Institute and served as director of the AHA's Kochhar Humanist Education Center from the beginning of 2008 to the end of 2013. I continue to serve as an educational consultant to the AHA.

Looking back from my vantage point at age eighty-three, I would say that I have been a humanist for as long as I can remember. Humanism for me is the most positive, life-affirming way of living imaginable. And the Ethical Culture affirmation of "Deed before Creed" sums up my approach to humanism very well!

But I should expand a bit on how I define humanism and why I think it is necessary.

To begin, humanism isn't the worship of humanity; it is the realization that humans have created many social, environmental, political, and other problems and that only humans can solve them. Some mythical earth-force won't do it for us. We're "home alone" on this planet, and one life is all we have, so we better make the best of it and improve our world while we are still part of it.

To do this, we need a different mindset. We need to refocus our efforts and spend our time and energy supporting, helping, and working with people of all kinds—and not just during crises like floods, tsunamis, and earthquakes, but all the time. And before this country enters any more wars, our leaders first need to ask themselves, "Are we sure there isn't a peaceful way of handling this situation?"

In our personal lives we shouldn't harm people with either our weapons or our words. While this is easier said than done, we should try to put ourselves in other people's shoes. The shoes may not fit exactly but we should try anyway. And we should try love the next time we are upset with someone. It has the same number of letters as the word hate but the results are much better.

Having such understandings and aspirations are why, many years ago, I realized that membership in a humanist organization was right for me. Relationships with fellow humans are more important than issues of whether or not we agree about the existence of a supreme being. Each of us should strive to help our children and grandchildren, as well as ourselves, develop and internalize a code of ethics to draw on when faced with difficult choices. Reason, compassion, and responsibility should be central to the way we strive to live.

Summing up, humanism affirms the worth, dignity, and uniqueness of every human being—even the ones with whom we disagree. This is my personal Humanist Manifesto.

❖

Rob Boston

Rob Boston is director of communications for Americans United for Separation of Church and State in Washington, DC, and the author of several books on church-state relations. A Pennsylvania native, Rob was raised Roman Catholic in a large family. He and his wife reside in Maryland. They have two children.

ૐ

was raised Roman Catholic and was pretty devout as a child. I attended a Catholic school for eight years and even considered joining the priesthood. Around age seventeen, however, I started having doubts. The articles of faith became harder for me to swallow. Catholics don't believe in interpreting the Bible literally, but they hold to certain mystical doctrines such as the virgin birth, transubstantiation, the Immaculate Conception, miracles, and the existence of saints. I did research and read books designed to explain it all, but my questions remained.

The more I read about science and history, the less I was able to keep believing in the supernatural. I was also turned off because in Catholicism the answer to doubts is too often "Just believe stronger" or "Puny human minds can't explain that yet." Such responses struck me as intellectually unsatisfying.

My transition to humanism was gradual. When I finally did leave the church I began calling myself an agnostic. A few years later I moved closer to atheism and then found humanism. Paul Kurtz's *Forbidden Fruit* was an important part of my journey. Prior to reading that book, I'd struggled with the idea of a truly secular ethic. Kurtz explained the concept so well, however, that I quickly realized, "This is what I am, and humanism is where I belong." Since some of my friends were already nonbelievers, my transformation was no big deal to them.

My family was another matter. I have five sisters and three brothers. Some remain Catholic while others have adopted different faiths. I'm sure a few were surprised when I abandoned religion entirely. I grew up in a conservative part of Pennsylvania where that sort of thing wasn't often done. You might leave the church of your youth, but you found another one. Or maybe you didn't attend a church regularly but you still believed in God. To drop religion entirely was pretty unusual.

My mother was very devout. The church meant a lot to her and provided comfort for her difficult life. I know she was disappointed when I left the faith, and it causes me pain to this day because I know that my embrace of humanism grieved her. She was a loving woman who worked hard with my father to raise a large family on a tight budget. She died in 2012, and I'm sure she was praying right up until the end that I would return to the fold.

Compared to when I was growing up, things are so much better now for young people grappling with these questions. When I was eighteen there was no Internet, and it could be difficult to even find information about humanism. In fact, I didn't know such a thing existed until I was in my twenties. So today I would urge people to take advantage of the resources available and learn from great humanist thinkers. Read their books, listen to them speak, attend humanist events, ask questions. Information is available at the speed of a mouse click. Take advantage of that.

I have offered the same advice to my two children. While it was never my goal to indoctrinate them in humanism, I did want to equip them with the tools of skepticism, healthy doubt of fantastic claims, and critical thinking. In our home, we had robust discussions about faith, religion, and God. I always encouraged my children to ask questions. My wife is Unitarian, and I had no problem with my daughter and son attending services and receiving religious training at her church, which is a very open and humanistic congregation. I'm pleased to say today that both of my children reflect humanist ethics.

Regarding humanism itself, I see it as encapsulating two key concepts. The first is the understanding that we are all part of an interconnected human family. We may choose to erect barriers of race, language, nationhood, and other divisions, but our common evolutionary ancestry binds us together and compels us to work as one for the betterment of all. The second is that our world is understandable and can be explained through science. Magic and the supernatural don't exist. And because there are no supernatural forces to turn to, we must find ways to solve our shared problems and work to create a system of ethics that isn't tied to ancient texts that some, but not others, deem holy.

Humanism rejects all forms of magical thinking and the supernatural—concepts that have worked their way into most religions. Humanism isn't defined by wishful thinking or appeals to mysterious forces. Rather, its platform is science, a self-correcting process that allows for change in the face of new evidence and information.

I don't recall how I first became aware of the American Humanist Association, but I have known of the group's work for some time. I see the AHA as a moderate body that labors to protect the rights of nonbelievers and to oppose prejudice against those who dare to doubt. I'm not interested in ridiculing beliefs that don't align with my own. Rather, I seek a society where freedom of conscience is absolute and the government doesn't presume to take sides on matters of theology. These are the values of the AHA as well.

❖

Lori Lipman **Brown**

Lori Lipman Brown served as the first director of the Secular Coalition for America from 2005-2009. A former Nevada state senator, lawyer, and educator, she currently works for an IT company in Virginia. Her early religious education in Queens, New York, was in Hebrew school at a Reform Judaism congregation. She and her spouse, Paul, are avid bicyclists.

G rowing up in Reform Judaism and later, at about age ten, in Unitarian Universalism, I didn't hear the word humanism (as a lifestance or philosophy) until my late teens. While my family was attending the Unitarian Universalist Congregation of Las Vegas, we decided to visit a Reform Judaism service to reconnect with our Jewishness. Being a Jew in New York was no big deal, but when we moved to Las Vegas, there was more emphasis on Christianity around us. So it made perfect sense to want to belong to the Jewish community. Our UU connections were more related to social justice work— which had become a central focus of UU congregations since the late 1960s—than the rituals there.

The Reform service was all about praising God. Participating in that sort of service was easy when I was a child going to Hebrew school. However, by the time we made this visit, each member of my immediate family (mother, father, brother, and I) had let go of supernatural beliefs and were all atheists. So when we got home, my father told me about Humanistic Judaism, a fairly new movement that had recently started and was going strong in places like Chicago but didn't have any congregations in Las Vegas. He had been getting their quarterly journals, and I glanced at a few. We wished there was a Humanistic Jewish congregation in town. But since there wasn't, we continued our active participation in the UU Congregation. In fact my father and I were frequent speakers at the UU church regarding Jewish holidays, traditions, and philosophies. We also led a number of services that focused on humanism or a humanist response to contemporary issues. We remained extremely active in the social justice arm of the congregation.

As an adult, my humanism played a large role in my career choices. During law school in Los Angeles in the early 1980s, I interned with the National Center for Immigrant Rights, representing El Salvadoran and Haitian political asylum seekers. I was convinced that saving each individual life was extremely important even if the situation in their home countries was beyond my grasp. (The Unitarian Universalist Association was a leader in that asylum movement.) When I graduated, I practiced in a number of areas, but I thought that practicing family law would give me an opportunity to do great things to help battered spouses. It did not, but it did speed my way to burnout, and I went back to school to become a teacher.

There I focused on at-risk students, and I loved teaching English to students who were just learning the language or recently mainstreaming in from special education classes. Teaching drama allowed me to work with young people whose creatively different demeanors endeared them to me. And teaching communications to the shyest of the shy led to years of thank-yous from former students whose careers and lives had been made easier by overcoming their fear of publicly expressing themselves.

I later had great experiences teaching at the college level, especially US Constitution, American History, and Women's Studies.

Back when I was a lawyer I'd been asked to run for public office. But now that I was a teacher, it became a more practical thing to do (and less of a pay cut from teacher to legislator than from lawyer to legislator.) I ran a grassroots campaign and became a Nevada state senator. During that time I passed four laws. The one I'm most proud of was repealing Nevada's "Crimes against Nature" law (the anti-gay consensual sex law). The US Supreme Court had set a precedent in the 1986 case of *Bowers v. Hardwick*, saying that those laws weren't unconstitutional (but they over-turned *Hardwick* in 2003 in *Lawrence v. Texas*.)

When I ran for reelection, my religion (as a Jew—not as a humanist or atheist) was used in a smear campaign that included four legislators lying about my patriotism and my activities during the 1993 session. Every rabbi in Las Vegas came to my defense. I fondly recall the Orthodox rabbi saying, "It doesn't matter what kind of Jew Lori is, she is a Jew and we stand with her." As the re-sult of a defamation lawsuit against the four legislators, I was even-tually able to clear my name, but it was my first real experience with anti-Semitism. During the mid-1990s, even when I walked door-to-door for other candidates, people started asking, "Is he Christian? Because I only vote for Christians." My reaction to the experience was to get much more involved in the Las Vegas Jew-ish Community, joining Jewish charitable organizations and a new "Reconstructionist" congregation that had an activist rabbi. So my spouse, who wasn't required to convert, and I became members of Valley Outreach Synagogue. We were thus heavily involved in social justice activism with both the synagogue and the UU church.

Reconstructionist Judaism fit me better than Reform, and I appreciated being a member of a Jewish congregation in light of the anti-Jewish sentiment I'd experienced. But Humanistic Judaism still would have fit better. My Reconstructionist rabbi, Dick Shackett, was still more theistic than I, but he was a great person and the congregation was especially active in LGBT and women's rights.

Being out of political office after my reelection defeat left me freer to give talks explicitly about my humanism and atheism. I especially recall an early talk I gave titled "Coming Out as a Humanist." I'd noticed so many parallels at the time between LGBT coming out and my own carefully selected disclosures of nontheism. I became involved with a new group of humanists and got to meet wonderful people like the late Clark Adams. My father was very active in these groups, and I would sometimes spend Sundays going from UU church to Las Vegas Humanists meetings. (One Friday night a month was still spent at Valley Outreach Synagogue, which only had services monthly.)

I had been looking for work in Washington, DC, for some time when the opportunity to become the first director of the Secular Coalition for America (SCA) arose. I jumped at the chance and had a fantastic three-and-a-half year experience. I worked out of an office in the basement of the American Humanist Association. My right-hand person, Ron Millar, kept the wheels turning, while I lobbied Congress and traveled the country speaking and fundraising. Fred Edwords was excellent at helping me prepare for my appearances on Bill O'Reilly's show and such. Annie Singer, the SCA's communications consultant at the time, helped to get me on *The Colbert Report*, and we practiced my opening line all the way to New York on the subway. I had the opportunity to meet many members of the US House of Representatives and Senate and wonderful religious allies who included me completely in their church-state separation coalitions. In short, I became a professional humanist and a nontheist who owned the label "atheist" because that was the category most discriminated against and disparaged at the time.

It was during my time at the SCA that I got to meet Sherwin Wine, the founder of Humanistic Judaism. His Society for

Humanistic Judaism joined the SCA. Thus the organization I'd heard about decades before and the movement I'd identified with all those years were now part of my work.

Referring to religion, people have asked me what I am. At one point my answer got quite lengthy: "I am an atheist who is a Humanistic Jewish Unitarian Universalist feminist." Most people looked confused with that answer but didn't ask for further explanation. But no matter how I've chosen to identify myself over the years, humanism has flowed through my entire life, even before I knew about it. I grew up in a family that always emphasized standing up against oppression, even when you're not a member of the targeted group. Concern for others was never based on fear of punishment or hope for reward in an afterlife. It was based in empathy, in conscience. This is humanism. It fits me well.

❖

Lucille **Cormier**

Lucille Cormier is a visiting professor in humanities at Fitchburg State University in Massachusetts, teaching courses in philosophy and world religions. Prior to this she served as executive director of North Central Court Services, a nonprofit court mediation service, and was appointed chief probation officer at Fitchburg District Court. She received her doctoral degree in philosophy at the University of Massachusetts Amherst.

℔

was raised in a conservative French Canadian Roman Catholic family with strong ties to the church. I attended Catholic schools from kindergarten through my master's degree. Doctoral study at the University of Massachusetts Amherst was my first experience with secular education. I was thirty-nine years old then, married to a man with a similar background, and our children were being raised in the church. I was about as unlikely a candidate for secular humanism as you could find.

Yet my path to humanism was set from the first in the Roman Catholic humanistic tradition where each person is believed to be one of God's children, gifted with a rational, immortal soul—indeed made in the very image and likeness of the creator. Blessed were the poor, the hungry, the disenfranchised, the sick. Kindness and compassion were the core virtues valued in the brand of Catholicism in which I was raised. Being humanistic was an essential part of being a good Catholic.

However, my path to *secular* humanism is quite another story. In my twenties I started struggling with the problem of evil: why God allows his children to suffer so wretchedly. I also had been studying the work of philosopher David Hume. His *Dialogues Concerning Natural Religion* became a springboard for the study of the philosophy of religion over the next two decades. But it was all an intellectual debate. I still went to church and accepted that a dark night of the soul was part of religious faith—perhaps especially so for religious intellectuals. Heck, if Bishop John Shelby Spong could maintain faith with all his doubts and criticisms, why couldn't I?

But it all unraveled quite undramatically one Sunday afternoon in my elderly mother's kitchen. Suffering from long-term, painful arthritis, depressed and anxious with the beginnings of dementia, she angrily announced that "the good lord don't give a damn." Not much of a theological statement but it had the effect of a bucket of cold water in terms of bringing the esoteric philosophical debates to a close. Of course the good lord didn't give a damn because there was no good lord. Period. End of discussion.

I've known since then that the puzzle of human life falls perfectly into place if you just toss out the extraneous God piece. I'd been trying to fit that piece in for years. It never fit. It doesn't fit. It's not part of the puzzle. So that's how I became a secular humanist.

My mother passed away a couple of years later. I attended her funeral mass. I never told her about my "conversion." It would have been unkind. She had enough to contend with without having to know that she'd precipitated her daughter into atheism. I didn't make any big announcements, and no one except an older brother, a born-again Christian, noticed or was concerned. My brother Don tried to debate me out of it, prayed for me, sent literature. But no one from the church came looking for me.

In terms of my own household, my middle child had already rebelled against going to church (isn't it always the middle child!), and my husband and I had stopped forcing any of the children to go. All three are now secular adults.

I don't think my decision made any great impact on others, but you can never know the full effect of your example. I do know that it affected my teaching. I teach a course in the philosophy of human nature. Part of it is a discussion of life's meaning, and one of the views we study is humanism. Many of my students have self-identified as secular humanists as a result of their study. One wrote to me in an email, "I have discovered through this course that I am a Humanist. . . . And I am grateful to have a 'Home.'" That pretty much says it all.

Some six or seven years after my "conversion" I was looking for a local atheist group that I could spend time with, sharing ideas and values. I wasn't too clear on the details. I didn't even know at the time that there was an official humanist organization. In any case, I was on the Internet and came across the Greater Worcester Humanists. The group looked interesting and seemed to fit what I was looking for. I went to a meeting and was impressed with the folks there and the agendas of meetings. This was a group of very bright, articulate people working to create a truly free and just society. I joined and began to see the scope of the secular movement in the United States. The American Humanist Association through its legal, educational, and charitable work embodies my humanistic and intellectual values.

To me, being a humanist means being hopeful. In the face of appallingly irrational and cruel behavior of humans towards each other, it means trusting that we can, as a species, be better. It's a belief that through education and political action we can be free and allow others to be free as well. It's a belief that science and technology can and will erase most of the ills that plague us: physical, emotional, and social. In the end, humanism is a faith in human nature.

What distinguishes humanism from other ways of thinking? How many ways are there of thinking? There's thinking logically, of course. There's thinking creatively. There's a kind of irrational thinking that's based on fear or prejudice or superstition. Humanists, I hope, would be given to logical and creative thinking. The irrational sort isn't worthy of us.

Lastly, here are several suggestions I would give others who now follow a path to humanism:

Be happy. Laugh. This is a great journey we're on.

Be angry. Be damned persistent. Albert Einstein said, "Three great forces rule the world: stupidity, fear, and greed." Humanism is out to defeat them all.

Use your specific talents to support humanism. Everyone has gifts. Some people are great speakers and leaders. Some are writers or organizers or wonderfully extroverted fundraisers. Some are teachers or scholars. Some are helpers. Some are awesome cheerleaders. And, on some days, the best we can contribute is a warm body standing in the background—not at all a trivial contribution.

❖

Fred **Edwords**

Fred Edwords was executive director of the American Humanist Association for fifteen years, editor of the Humanist *magazine for twelve, and national director of the United Coalition of Reason for six. He also served as the first president of Camp Quest. He is now director of planned giving for the Humanist Foundation of the American Humanist Association.*

T he year was 1954—when everybody believed in God and Davy Crockett—when suburban children walked hand-in-hand to the corner church for Sunday school, carrying the weekly pledge offering their non-attending parents sent with them—when people were expected to be Christian, preferably Mainline Protestant, but not to wear it on their sleeves—and when I received my perfect attendance button in front of the whole congregation at my neighborhood church in San Diego, California. This was my world: conventional, wholesome, and conformist. And it stayed that way through most of the Eisenhower administration.

But then the 1960s blossomed. New ideas were in the air. School teachers, friends, and my older brother challenged me on a lot of things. One summer I engaged in a personal study of comparative mythology, gave up the Bible because of it, and yawned my way out of the United Methodist Church. During college I passed effortlessly from deism to atheism and started reading Thomas Paine and Robert Ingersoll.

But I hung onto the notion that psychic phenomena were real. Completely taken in by the television series *One Step Beyond* and assorted books, I viewed the scientific study of the paranormal as promising the best explanation for religion's mysteries, miracles, and spiritual experiences. I figured that when science got to the bottom of all this and discovered the secret forces at work, religion would fall by the wayside as obsolete. With more reading, however, and useful conversations with others, I was gradually disabused of such thinking.

By the mid-1970s I had become aware of the rise of humanism. This was the heady time of Humanist Manifesto II and the plethora of high-profile humanist statements that followed it, signed by leading thinkers from around the world. The American Humanist Association was famous. My intellectual friends and I became energized by this and joined the Humanist Association of San Diego, an AHA chapter.

Then we became alarmed by the rise of creationism. So we began studying the creationist arguments, researching the answers, and two of us prepped for a big public debate against Henry Morris and Duane Gish of the Institute for Creation Research. After the excitement of that jointly-sponsored humanist-creationist event in 1978, with its raucous overflow audience, my friends and I were hooked and soon launched a quarterly journal called *Creation/Evolution*.

By this time I was not only a chapter leader but coordinator of all AHA West Coast chapters. A team of us put on a regional conference. And then the AHA suddenly hired me to run its national office, located at that time in Amherst, New York, a suburb of blizzardy Buffalo. Thus began—on July 1, 1980—a thirty-five year career in humanism.

During the 1980s, while running the AHA and editing *Creation/Evolution* (which became an AHA publication), I emerged to be what creationists disparagingly dubbed "an anti-creationist hired gun," one of a small cadre of speakers specially prepared to debate leading creationists at colleges and universities all across the country. Our efforts disrupted the creationist gambit of finding unsuspecting college professors who they could publicly blindside with their pseudoscientific chicanery. But by 1990 I was satisfied with the success of this work and soon arranged to have *Creation/Evolution* sold to the National Center for Science Education, an organization I'd helped organize. There the journal remained in publication for many years more.

But let's step back a bit. In my personal life, I used landing my AHA job in 1980 as the cue to get married. So my wife Mary and I had a humanist wedding in San Diego. Then, after a brief honeymoon in Palm Springs, I left for Buffalo while she wrapped up her personal affairs so she could join me later. This was when a totally unexpected drama exploded.

Mary's mother lured her on a sudden trip to Arkansas to visit a relative who was apparently dying. But that was just a ruse to put Mary into the hands of a hired deprogrammer who aimed to remove her from the "cult of secular humanism." Since Mary had become an atheist on her own before I'd met her, and we'd been together four-and-a-half years before we got married, she had the intellectual and emotional roots to endure a harrowing week before the deprogrammer gave up and another week before her family did. Mary and her mother then flew back to San Diego, Mary was greeted at the airport by the local humanists I'd mobilized, she got her affairs in order (after more tribulations), and then flew to Buffalo, where she and I reunited.

It took a few years, and two children, before that broken fence in her own family could finally be mended.

Our first daughter was born in 1984 and the second in 1986. Having children put my humanist ideas to the test. For you see, it's one thing to acquire humanist ideas by abandoning something else—I knew how to do that. It's quite another to grow up humanist —this I had no experience with and knew no one who had. Yet this is what I wanted to help my daughters do.

I'd long since given up my hard atheist position of the early 1970s when I'd viewed the universe as so constituted that there was no possibility of a god. Now, influenced by Logical Positivism, I saw the god idea as meaningless and therefore neither true nor false. To give that position a label, I'd adopted Rabbi Sherwin Wine's term *Ignostic*. But how would I ever explain Logical Positivism to a child?

Thus I opted for silence, deciding to test the hypothesis put forth by many evangelicals, and believed by some humanists, that the god idea is a natural-occurring notion that children's minds will gravitate to on their own, even if they are never exposed to it externally. Well, each of my daughters got all the way to first grade without any godly notions. Then, in the case of the eldest, some pushy kid preached to her, and she came home wanting to know what this scary new business was about. Suddenly on the spot, I used Socratic cross-examination to ask her what she thought it all meant, helping her to see that this stuff made no sense. And the bit that did make sense—the big-guy-in-the-sky (who actually does carry falsifiable meaning)—was without supporting evidence. I asked her if she'd ever seen anything like that. She said no. I said I hadn't either. (We'd both flown in airplanes without ever noticing a big guy up there.) Then I told her that a lot of people believed such things anyway, but our family was one of the few that didn't accept something just because others did. That put an end to the god question for her (since the abstract god of the theologians never made any sense). It was similar for our youngest daughter, who became quite laid-back and passive about the whole matter. Then, when unexpectedly pressed in high school, she actually stumped her guidance counselor with the "Who created God?" rejoinder.

Meanwhile, back in my professional life, the membership of the American Humanist Association, after doubling by the end of the 1980s, enjoyed a continuous rise through the 1990s. To further enhance the AHA's growing role in the secular movement, I became a counselor at Camp Quest, the secular summer camp, serving for eleven years. And when the camp incorporated in 2002, I became its first corporate president.

But I knew the AHA wasn't going to truly break out and become a significant force in the world until it could place its headquarters in the nation's capital. So, working from the solidity of the organization's sound financial footing, I convinced the board of directors that it was time to make the move. As part of that process, I agreed to let a new executive director, Tony Hileman—who had Washington, DC, savvy—take over the helm as I shifted my role to purely editorial, taking charge of all of the organization's publications. A few years later, after Roy Speckhardt succeeded Hileman, I shifted my role to public relations, managing the AHA's first controversial bus ad campaign, which got me an appearance on *The O'Reilly Factor* and other shows.

Then the AHA helped bring the United Coalition of Reason into existence. I became this new organization's first director, serving from 2009 through 2014, spreading billboard and bus ad campaigns across the nation. Finally, after helping to hire and train my successor, I went into semi-retirement as director of planned giving for the Humanist Foundation (the AHA's endowment fund). Looking back I can say I've enjoyed a full life as a humanist activist, and am now preparing for my next adventure.

❖

Rebecca Newberger **Goldstein**

Dr. Goldstein is a philosopher and novelist, and the author of ten books of both fiction and nonfiction, including 36 Arguments for the Existence of God: A Work of Fiction *and* Plato at the Googleplex: Why Philosophy Won't Go Away. *She is a MacArthur Fellow and a member of the American Academy of Arts and Sciences. She was named Humanist of the Year by the American Humanist Association in 2011 and awarded the National Humanities Medal by President Obama in 2015.*

𝕌

was brought up in an Orthodox Jewish family. This identity
—and it was emphatically presented to me as constituting
my identity—was meant to script my life. My gender was an
all-important feature in this script. I was brought up to have no
ambitions beyond getting married at an early age and then having
children.

Certain aspects of my personality made this script uncomfortable. For one thing, I had pronounced ambitions, mostly in an academic direction. (Fortunately, although I went to a very backward
all-girls religious high school, I did receive standardized testing,
which got me into a good college.) For another, I reacted negative-
ly to the implied message that people can be characterized by the
group into which they happen to be born. Taking responsibility
for our own beliefs seemed among the most important of our human responsibilities. So group essentialism struck me as not only
intellectually incoherent but also morally repellent. And last, as
an impediment to the life script I'd been handed, was the fact
that I became an agnostic in adolescence and an atheist in early
adulthood.

Interestingly, the last of these considerations was the least important in my gradual identification as more a humanist than a
Jew. For after becoming an atheist I lived for decades strictly ob-

serving the Jewish traditions of my family. Breaking them would have broken my parents' hearts, a move that seemed forbidden by the very humanism I'd embraced. So I tried to carve out a compromise that wouldn't leave me feeling hypocritical. What this meant was that I kept all the laws of Orthodoxy, as extraordinarily inconvenient as they were, while also telling my family that I didn't keep them out of conviction but out of respect and love for them. Their attitude was that I'd eventually come around; the mere habitual performance of all the rituals would induce belief. And if it didn't happen that way, they'd be satisfied with my observance. In Orthodox Judaism, behavior trumps belief.

And observe I did, finally giving it all up only after both my parents had died. I was forty-nine years old then, which is quite a few decades of living as an Orthodox Jewish atheist. There was still the rest of my family to consider, including my siblings, but I figured they could deal with it, which most of them have. I at last had earned the right to live as I believed, just as the rest of my family lived as they believed. (The lack of symmetry is something to consider. None of them would have thought it tolerable to be forced to live, say, by my beliefs.) I left every aspect of observance behind. I have no vestige of attachment to the traditions and rituals that characterized the majority of my life and reject any identification that essentializes an arbitrary fact about me.

I occasionally will hear from a cousin who will try to impress on me the illogic of not believing in "G-d." Orthodox Jews believe the tetragrammaton YHWH is so holy that it can't be spoken or written, and extend this prohibition to even the English word "God." This past autumn one such email invoked Einstein and his famous phrase that "G-d doesn't play dice with the world." Physicists often resort to God-talk as a cute way of formulating their intuitions concerning the ultimate laws of nature; the language does a world of harm. After trying to explain what Einstein meant by that phrase, and why it shouldn't be interpreted as implying any theistic commitments, I went on to express my usual response when confronted with people who try to batter me into belief.

> I'm not interested in talking you out of your religion. I credit you with having given thought to your beliefs. I only ask that you credit me with having done the same to my beliefs. I happen to believe that we'll never all agree, since a lot of the deepest disagreements involving the nature of reality and our place within it derive from temperamental differences. Where both rational argument and empirical evidence fall short of forcing a conclusion, temperamental characteristics rush in to fill the vacuum. The difference between those who can tolerate this diversity of beliefs and those who can't cuts across the boundary between believers and nonbelievers. I think that the former difference is more important than the latter.

It has been, to say the least, a liberating experience to finally be able to come out and say exactly what I believe and to live exactly as I think those beliefs dictate. But even more emotionally powerful for me is the great closeness this allows me to feel with people whose backgrounds could not have been more different from mine. This is particularly poignant when those backgrounds were as religious as my own—only the religion was evangelical Protestant or Catholic or Muslim or Hindu. It's a bonding experience to hear how, though the starting points have been antagonistically different from each other, the steps that led us to our same humanist conclusions were almost identical, because it was reason that was determining the trajectory.

This experience, which always moves me beyond words, bears out a point made by Baruch Spinoza. Reason, he predicted, offers us the sweetness of being able to share in each other's point of view in the most expansive way possible, which changes our very identity. Our identity should never be something we passively inherit but rather something we actively acquire, our lifelong project. And to the extent that we commit ourselves to reason, then, no matter where we start out in this project, we'll draw closer to partaking in the same identity, the human identity—a goal that offers a succinct way to express the essence of humanism.

But to elaborate a bit more on how I understand humanism: It's a moral system that makes no supernatural assumptions but rather grounds and explicates the moral life by appealing only to natural facts. It's the normative face of naturalism. The natural facts appealed to are those about human nature, specifically these:

(1) Each individual is committed to her or his own wellbeing and flourishing. (Spinoza called this commitment *conatus*).

(2) We humans are, in some essential sense, social. Aspects that make us who we are, for example our language instinct, are explicable only within the context of a community.

(3) We are reason-giving creatures, who not only act and believe but also offer reasons for our actions and beliefs (though not necessarily good ones).

It's from these empirical facts that humanism derives its powerful commitment to the flourishing of all human life, whether it exists now or in the generations to come (which demands that we assume stewardship of our planet).

It was Plato who articulated a powerful argument demonstrating that morality cannot be soundly established on theistic grounds. Plato's so-called Euthyphro argument has been repeated by freethinkers throughout the generations, from Spinoza to Bertrand Russell. The conclusion of Plato's argument should be read as a disjunction: Either there is a nontheistic source for grounding morality or there is no morality at all. What humanism demonstrates is the viability of the first disjunct, producing a morality which, utilizing nothing more than the facts of human nature, produces the most expansive of moral outlooks, minimizing the differences between us, maximizing our responsibilities toward each other, widening and strengthening the adaptive inclination toward empathy while weakening the adaptive inclination toward xenophobia.

And this brings me to the importance of the American Humanist Association. America is an outlier among prosperous Western nations in remaining largely ignorant of the vitality of the first disjunct of Plato's conclusion. This ignorance has the unfortunate consequence of producing moral outlooks that are anything but expansive. It also produces lawmakers who, intent on legislating morality, assault the separation between church and state, perverting the Enlightenment philosophy of the founders. The American Humanist Association pushes back against this perversion. And the association takes care of us in other ways, providing a community in which we can experience the sweetness that Spinoza had promised those who pursue the goals of reason and human flourishing.

❖

Han Hills

Han Hills has been a humanist celebrant based in North Carolina since 2006. He is an author, teacher, podcaster, and small business owner. He helped create the first Carolinas Secular Conference and also cofounded the Carolinas Secular Association.

was raised in a family that was almost entirely secular. My parents taught me that moral values consisted in caring, kindness, and personal responsibility. My mother identified as an atheist, although she was always careful to tell me, even as a young child, that I should seek out my own belief system. It was important to her that I was shown the value of an open mind. I like to think this provided fertile ground for the positive perspective and rationality of humanist thinking.

Growing up in England, I encountered what seemed to be the flaccid vestiges of an unenthusiastic spirituality. School assemblies were often cold and tedious affairs, running through dull, repetitive routines and rituals. These felt like the continuous loops of a fading tape recording, growing weaker and more garbled with each passing year. The meaning of the words we were required to parrot had no direct or personal relevance to the experiences and problems I encountered each day. Similarly, on the rare "seasonal" occasions we were marched into a chilly stone chapel, where we found ourselves surrounded mostly by an older, tired generation. Amid the dampness and the rosewater, it seemed that those gathered weren't there through passionate belief but rather by habit. Worse, it may well have been a niggling fear of approaching mortality. All these occasions found no meaning in my heart, and I now believe this response is shared by a great many of my generation across Britain.

If experiences such as these cannot touch or connect with our lives, this would seem to present a bottomless sinkhole in the path of an increasingly moribund Church of England.

My road to humanism didn't take me through any moments of blinding revelation. Rather, it contained regular sparks of instruction and measured realization. I came to believe that, constantly and consistently throughout life, one must seek new experiences and listen carefully to all viewpoints. Growth in understanding can only be fueled by taking fresh steps and breathing new air. It is not encountered by walking in narrow circles of intellectual safety or maintaining blind acceptance of old opinions.

Although I have stayed close to the family outlook with which I began, the more I have developed my humanist thinking, the more I have realized that the importance of any spiritual perspective goes beyond debates about the supernatural or the existence of a deity. I have come to believe that it is far more important to focus on social, environmental, and practical concerns. I left behind a narrow tradition regarding religion that was centered only on an adversarial position to faith, and have found a philosophy that focuses on leading by practical and positive example in all aspects of life. Even in our failings we can provide valuable lessons to ourselves and others.

Although most people close to me have embraced humanism as a new and fascinating viewpoint, I have seen an initial cautious skepticism when first introducing it to strangers. However, once I have explained the core values of empathy, curiosity, and positivity, I have almost always found others reacting with increasing enthusiasm. I believe it is very difficult to be critical of any outlook based on care for others and our world.

My first advice to anyone seeking to understand humanism is to always keep an open mind. Ours is a philosophy of discovery.

When we seek and carefully evaluate all the possibilities of outlook, however strange, we illuminate our world. With that knowledge comes an ever-increasing drive and ability to change all our lives for the better. This is the core of my humanism and must surely form the center of all human behavior if we are to thrive as a species.

I have encountered several men and women who have become disenchanted and frustrated by a repetitive, and often hypocritical, faith tradition. Unfortunately, many feel unable to express their doubts, often because of the dangers of social ostracization. I have been told that my own open skepticism, and vocal counter-opinions, has given some a little more courage to express this openly to those in their lives. If I have helped even one individual take a small step to a happier personal expression, I can think of no more fortunate and valuable way to have invested my time.

For me, the core of humanism is about empathy. Instead of seeing ourselves as singular, or only an embattled faction, I hope we can see ourselves as part of, and equal to, all of humanity. I also believe this should be extended to a passionate care for all life. We must take a firm, and personal, responsibility for our world. Humanism motivates us to do these things, not from some hope of a vague posthumous compensation, but for the daily reward of building a world that increases real and measurable happiness for all.

Humanism stands as a truly open system of thought. Unrestrained by any absolute creed, or ancient sacred texts, the experience of humanism offers opportunities for intellectual discovery and emotional growth limited only by our willingness and energy. It doesn't seek to dictate, control, or exploit, but rather to encourage a critical freedom, holding the values of personal growth above all.

Unlike most religious viewpoints, humanism is an entirely positive philosophy, devoid of destructive and negative concepts such as sin, damnation, and the terrible personal restrictions of repressive doctrines.

As for the American Humanist Association, which I discovered through my involvement in a local humanist community, I truly admire the way it works tirelessly to promote the freedoms and liberties of self-expression, and the way it educates us all on the paramount importance of a free and open quest for knowledge.

❖

Sikivu Hutchinson

Sikivu Hutchinson is the author of Moral Combat: Black Atheists, Gender Politics, and the Values Wars; Godless Americana: Race and Religious Rebels; *and the novel* White Nights, Black Paradise. *She is the founder of Black Skeptics Los Angeles and the Women's Leadership Project, a feminist mentoring program for high school girls of color. She is also a senior fellow for the Institute for Humanist Studies.*

grew up in a secular household and never had to transition from being religious to humanist. I subscribe to radical humanism as a worldview and belief system.

To me, radical humanism means that religious hierarchies of race, gender, sexuality, and class are harmful to universal human rights and the self-determination of oppressed peoples. Radical humanism in communities of color seeks to allow nonbelievers of color cultural legitimacy, visibility, and validity in the midst of an often hostile worldview that says there is only one way to be black or Latino and that women and the LGBTQ community are marginal or aberrant. Radical humanism recognizes the inalienable human rights of all people to an equitable education, shelter, food, affordable health care, a clean, violence-free environment, and a living-wage job. It recognizes women's inalienable right to self-determination vis-à-vis reproductive choice, abortion on demand, and family planning free of state intervention, authority, and control. It recognizes the inherent morality of love between two consenting adults of all sexual orientations and genders as well as the value of LGBTQ and gender nonconforming identities. This version of humanism is distinguished from other belief systems insofar as there are no judgments, hierarchies, and privileged regimes of knowledge that stratify groups and individuals based on Eurocentric binaries.

For those transitioning to humanism I'd recommend trying to find a culturally responsive community organization with a secular orientation. The American Humanist Association has provided greater visibility to a range of issues that transcend the traditional secular-atheist, church-state separation, and science emphasis. The organization is still growing in its efforts to represent a more racially and ethnically diverse community of humanists and nonbelievers.

Recently, the AHA joined several other secular organizations in supporting and promoting the 2016 Secular Social Justice (SSJ) conference which brought together atheists/humanists of color, activists, educators, and writers from around the country. The SSJ conference is currently the only national space for humanists of color to make presentations on and discuss critical social justice issues pertaining to racism, economic justice, feminism, queer rights, and the agency of people of color in the secular movement. Of course, these issues cut across boundaries of secular and religious, and are among the most important to the everyday lives of people of color.

However, it's critical for the mainstream humanist movement to understand that progressive secular African-American folk, for example, will not jump on the humanist bandwagon simply because a given organization publicly aligns with a cause or causes important to our communities. Long-term coalition building that's effective will come when a greater number of people of color have positions of power in secular organizations (such as management positions where they're able to greenlight funding for programming, advocate for policy initiatives that impact communities of color on the local and national level, as well as advance a national platform of equity and racial justice) and are able to grow and sustain self-determining organizations that provide economically and socially viable alternatives to organized religion.

❖

Arthur **Jackson**

Art Jackson has been active in the American Humanist Association since 1962. In 1963 he attended the AHA's first training session to provide humanist celebrants for weddings and other ceremonies and has worked as its assistant executive director, coordinating AHA's celebrant and chapter programs. He is the author of The Humanist Chapter of the Future and the Future of Humanism *(1982, revised 1993) and* How to Live the Good Life: A User's Guide for Modern Humans *(2011). He is a former president and current member of the Humanist Society board of directors.*

I was born into a nominally Christian Protestant family in the early 1930s. However, there was not much involvement in churches since my mother, my primary caregiver, was anti-clerical.

However, as I got older, there was some Sunday school activity which I found to be unpleasant. Since my family moved a great deal, I attended churches of several different varieties of Protestantism. This became important as I pondered a core message they each expressed: "We are right. All others are wrong. We go to heaven. Everyone else goes to hell."

Eventually I realized that they couldn't all be right. But they could all be wrong, especially since none of them had a reasonable claim to the correctness of their position. Nonetheless I wanted to find a community I could be part of and draw guidance from. Since this was in the days before the Internet, searching out answers was a difficult process. So I read every book I could find that might help me.

Where I grew up it appeared that everyone was Christian. I struggled with this since, if rejecting Christianity was the obvious answer, why was I the only one doing it? Something seemed wrong with this picture, which left me feeling that my thinking was on a shaky foundation. This made my steps forward difficult, punctuated with steps backward.

Although in middle school I became convinced there was no God, it took only a few months to realize that if there is no God, now what? And it was the "now what" question that powered my efforts to understand what the world and life were all about.

In college I explored other options like Unitarianism. But somehow what went on in those churches wasn't satisfying to me. Then in my senior year, as part of a philosophy assignment, I was led to find Corliss Lamont's book, *The Philosophy of Humanism*. Even though I quibbled with some of the things he wrote, it was a boost to my peace of mind to discover there were other people in the world like me and they called themselves humanists.

Because humanism fit me so well, that's what I've been calling myself ever since. But at that time nothing I had learned had made me, aware there was an organized humanist movement populated by others with whom I could connect. It would take several years to find that.

In the meantime I began working to record all the diverse elements of the ideas I ran across so as to tie them together into a coherent whole. My college philosophy class provided the foundation for doing this, and I wrote an essay on ethics in which the meaning of life was the core idea.

Because I had gone to college on an NROTC scholarship, I had three years of active duty in the US Marine Corps after my graduation. During that time I was stationed for a while in Japan, where I decided to have "humanism" stamped on my dog tags. (There have been many moves in my life since then, so unfortunately I no longer have them to proudly display.)

After my period in the service I taught junior high school science and math. During that time I came across an article in a 1962 *Time* magazine about a conference of the International Humanist and Ethical Union in the Netherlands. The article mentioned that there was a humanist organization in the United

States, the American Humanist Association, headquartered in Yellow Springs, Ohio. I wrote to them and that year became a card-carrying member.

Since there was a very active affiliate of the AHA in Portland, Oregon, near where I was teaching, I started attending their weekly meetings. From that connection I eventually came to work for the AHA in Yellow Springs, serving as assistant executive director.

It was there that I came up with my own definition of humanism: "Humanism is the belief that human beings are the source of meaning and value and their morality comes naturally out of our evolutionary history." The epiphany—coming out of the blue—that produced my definition was in response to a visitor's question, but it provided an answer that I myself had been looking for since getting involved in organized humanism. I had never considered these words before. But after hearing them I decided that the definition was perfect.

In 1969 I moved to San Jose, California, to experiment with the model of having a paid administrator for an AHA chapter. The Humanist Community of San Jose thrived for a few years under that plan, but around 1976 funding for my position was severely reduced and I went to work for the County of Santa Clara. That job gave me enough free time to nurture the chapter back to life and manage the AHA's celebrant program. It ultimately provided the retirement funds to allow me to continue my humanist activism into the twenty-first century.

All this time I was working to tie my own thinking together within the humanist framework. I put this in a manuscript I was developing from my college essay on the meaning of life. My aim was to establish a foundation on which a scientifically-based ethical system or religion could be erected.

This effort culminated in my book, *How to Live the Good Life: A User's Guide for Modern Humans,* which I published in 2011 following decades of effort to bring it to a stopping point. I finally realized it could never be finished because it was open to change and development as new knowledge and new understandings came to my awareness.

However, by recognizing that human beings are for us the ultimate reference system, it became possible for me to focus on the fact that our individual lives are what is most important. I realized that living at the highest level that current circumstances allow is the goal, and that developing local humanist groups to bring people together is an important part of this. It became clear to me that the foregoing must be at the core of all of our efforts and that all other knowledge needs to support this. That is what my humanism has brought me to.

❖

Margaret Placentra **Johnston**

As a practicing optometrist, Dr. Johnston has spent the last three decades helping people see better in the physical world. But now she is on a new mission to offer clearer vision of a different sort: a broader perspective about religion and spirituality than what the conventional world typically recognizes. Her book, Faith Beyond Belief: Stories of Good People Who Left Their Church Behind, *was named a 2013 Nautilus Book Award Gold Winner. She has two grown sons and lives with her husband in Northern Virginia.*

I was born into a nominally Catholic family. Throughout my childhood my siblings and I were taught to say our prayers before bed and were sent to Mass on Sundays and Catholic school during the week.

In elementary school we were handed all the facts of our religion in a neat little book called the catechism. We were led to believe that everything about our religion had already been figured out by others and all we had to do was memorize it and then, of course, follow the rules. Nothing about the religion I knew in my youth inspired any sense of feeling or connection. It seemed to be a rote matter inspired mainly by the expectation that we conform to family and cultural norms. Going to church was just something "people like us" did.

In high school things became more interesting. We were let in on the secret that a lot of the catechism answers we had so rigorously memorized were not literally true. There was no actual place up in the sky where good people were rewarded and no place beneath the earth where a fiery devil lurked to administer eternal punishment to the bad ones. Heaven and hell were merely states of existence, and when they said Jesus was the son of God, that was just anthropomorphic language, something the religious authorities had made up so common folk could understand a complex concept. Even the Bible stories were allegorical, they told us, not historically valid representations. Well, this was news!

Despite a mild sense of irritation that the grade school nuns had made us spend years memorizing things that weren't true, I was delighted we were finally going to be let in on the real truth. But unfortunately, in the subsequent religion classes, we moved on to cover things like comparative religions, family life, and the like. They never did get around to telling us the real truths about Catholicism. And for me, without all those facts and rules, I didn't know what the Catholic Church was all about. So I chose to study religion at a higher level in college.

At the Catholic University of America, all the theology classes encouraged us to question church tenets and to reason out our beliefs on our own. For me, the end result of all the questioning was that most Catholic teachings, as I understood them at the time, did not stand up to rational examination.

I finished college as a confirmed, proud atheist. I was certain that all the time and effort people expended in assuring their salvation through church participation could be better spent focusing on the practical aspects of the here and now and, where possible, in helping others. In fact, I was very happy to be freed from some of the really scary parts of the Catholic religion: the devil and the threats of eternal punishment in hell.

Most of all, I decided that if I were to live a good life, it would be up to me to figure out how; morality was not a matter of confessing my sins in time. How about if I just lived by a higher standard and didn't do wrong things? What if I avoided doing the things that I knew in my heart were wrong simply because it felt better to do the right thing? Living this way, I wouldn't need to concern myself with eternal punishment or reward. I didn't even believe there was any life after death anyway.

I also decided that the only thing that counted was the here and now: life right here on earth was an incredible gift, and if I took every opportunity to make this life the best I possibly could, then no possible God "up there" (if, by chance, there was an afterlife) could fault me for the use I had made of that gift. I would determine my life's course and, as long as I followed my own conscience, I would always know I had done my best.

Years later, I found my way to humanism when I was looking for some form of values training for my two boys. I couldn't send them to any religious Sunday school because I couldn't back up anything they would be taught there. My search led me to the Northern Virginia Ethical Society. Here I found open-minded and open-hearted people who I was happy to have educating my children. They espoused values very similar to the ones I had arrived at during my college years of searching. Many or most had gone through a questioning and reasoning process similar to mine regarding the truth of their birth religion and I felt comfortable among these like-minded people.

Just recently I have learned of the work of the evolutionary theologian Michael Dowd. Light years ahead of your typical Christian minister, Dowd defines religion as a person's search to be in "right relationship to reality." This means that a person embraces the human reasoning process and our modern scientific findings like the average humanist. But she or he also senses a connection with those who don't do this and chooses not to ignore concepts that don't fit the scientific paradigm.

As someone who has put a great deal of effort into studying religious belief versus nonbelief, I want to say that there is one thing we can be sure of: the more inclusive a person is, the broader and more comprehensive the worldview they can embrace, the more integrated they are.

Dowd's theology can be called post-critical, to be contrasted against the pre-critical worldview of the typical religious believer and the critical worldview of the typical nonbeliever. Today there exist a host of newly emerging post-critical thinkers who call us to welcome animals, plants, and the ecosystem into our worldview, as many humanists already do.

But they also challenge us toward something more: to not shut down the questioning process after that first critical step beyond traditional belief. They provide a rationale for humanists and the like to permanently open hearts and minds to further questioning and to broaden worldviews beyond what can be proven by science. This might allow us to notice, for example, intuition when it arises in our consciousness. Right relationship to reality wouldn't allow us to dismiss out of hand the knowledge we obtain intuitively. But where would intuition be coming from that science cannot explain?

Post-critical thinkers describe a highly sophisticated worldview devoid of supernatural connotations and devoid of simplistic explanations about how we got here or where we are going. It is a philosophy (or even a spirituality) which includes humanism but also transcends it, encompassing everyone and everything—including messy concepts like intuition and others we don't have scientific answers for yet.

It even makes way for a more generous and more kindly interpretation of what religions are about. Despite the fact that each religion claims to supply ultimate truth, the post-critical worldview allows a person to see past this provincialism. A post-critical thinker will forgive religions their lack of literal veracity out of respect for the overarching phenomenon that unites them all, a human need we all share: the desire to establish a right relationship to reality. So I now stretch myself to include into my worldview even bigger questions, and the inevitable uncertainties of life's mysteries.

❖

Marissa Torres **Langseth**

Marissa Torres Langseth is an adult nurse practitioner and founder of HAPI, the Humanist Alliance Philippines, International.

ⅠⅠ

n the Philippines, children are baptized as Roman Catholic as early as three to six months old. It was the same for me. During my childhood I was forced to practice that Catholicism by threats and physical injury. My mother would wake me up Sunday mornings with kicks and slaps to ensure that I wasn't late for church.

To my parents' thinking, everything came from God: "We have to be thankful that we are alive because God gave us life" and so forth. All of the answers anyone needed were "from God." So I just went with the flow to keep my mother and father off my back, since at that time in the Philippines one needed to follow parents and authority figures.

But in the fifth grade, at age eleven, after science was introduced in my class, I started to become skeptical. I began asking lots of questions which no one could answer. Then as a teenager I joined the church choir. I was still subservient then, looking up to authorities, following orders from my parents, and believing that men should be the leaders and women are secondary citizens.

During my first year of college I was almost raped by a military priest. But I was a fast runner back then and escaped.

In 1990 I came to the United States as a registered nurse. Once here I desperately needed to find a group right for me, to find a home. So I joined church groups, was even born again. But something always seemed to be lacking, and many questions remained in my mind. This ongoing skepticism resulted in my not having many friends.

But in my capacity as a registered nurse, serving in an emergency room and later in a nursing home, I conducted a private little experiment. Seeing a lot of dying people, I spoke with them and asked if they would contact me after death if there really was an afterlife. So far I haven't heard back from anyone.

Later, in 2010—after having lived in a largely covert mode for many years, avoiding active discussion of my thoughts—I joined Facebook and began debating with religious people. This became a way of letting out my frustrations about religion, especially after 9/11. I even convinced all but one of my sisters to change their minds. Almost half of my classmates from high school and college, however—even those who knew me well or who I had assisted financially—became unfriendly. This only made my passion grow, and I wanted to change people's thinking and make a difference.

During this time I knew I was atheistic but didn't know what to actually call myself. So I started researching online, found the American Humanist Association, labeled myself a humanist, and became a member. Then on February 14, 2011, I became the first person in the Philippines to create a group of atheists and humanists that was registered and legal to function. This was the Philippine Atheists and Agnostics Society (PATAS). Later that year I attended my first AHA conference, meeting Richard Dawkins, other speakers, and the AHA staff. I thought, "Hey, these are real humans, real people, who want to improve the world. I'm with them!"

But I left PATAS in November 2013 and in December organized HAPI, which stands for the Humanist Alliance Philippines, International. The group went public online on January 1, 2014, with a greeting of "HAPI New Year."

Today HAPI is a nonprofit community of progressive secular humanists from all over the world with common goals for the greater good of humanity. Although we work on an international basis, our primary focus is directed toward the Philippines. Our members come from different social sectors in various countries and aim to promote democratic values and defend every person's right to personal and collective freedom. HAPI works for equality, for protection of children from violence and exploitation, and against poverty and discrimination.

Our vision is of a world that champions humanism through common sense, reason, and logic. And our mission, with our international allies, is to awaken the Filipino people to share and practice the same vision, ensure church-state separation, end religious privilege in the Philippines, and promote the idea that only people can help people, that only humanity can save humanity.

We will:

- work in harmony with any institution (religious or non-religious) for the betterment of humanity

- stand and fight, through peaceful discussion and dialogue, for equal rights for all human beings, unrestricted by religious or political doctrine or dogma

- help those in need, regardless of religion, nonbelief, or political ideology

- promote science, logic, and empathy as guiding lights toward humanity's morality and evolution

- openly question and expose the inequalities of religious and political ideology that continue to needlessly divide humankind toward the end of uniting all people in one common human family.

My passion in all of this is to "pay it forward" and make a difference. I am a humanist. I am an atheist. I believe that only human beings can make the world better. I am not afraid.

❖

Nancy **Martin**

Currently retired, Nancy Martin serves on the board of directors of the Secular Student Alliance and on the advisory board for Red Butte Gardens. Previously she was on the board of the Evolution Institute. Nancy enjoyed three careers: as a professor of computer science, executive in her own small business and in larger international companies, and partner at Warburg Pincus. She was also active in the drive to get more women in science and engineering, cofounding in the early 1970s the still-thriving New Mexico Network for Women in Science and Engineering. She has two children and four grandchildren.

lthough I grew up in a Mormon household and community, I was an atheist from the age of seven because, even to my young mind, the theology made no sense. So it was only out of respect for my parents that I attended church regularly, having a 100 percent attendance record for years. Moreover, up to the age of seventeen, I had only met two non-Mormons, and they were Catholic. So from what I could see there was no other course to take than silence.

There were, however, two experiences that were "confirmational."

The first was when I was undergoing the requisite baptismal ritual at age eight. My braids refused to be submerged. On the third try, the elder wrapped them around my wrist so they would go down. I was pleased that my hair had offered the resistance which I could not.

The second experience was at a meeting called "Mutual." A group of about fifty young women, ages twelve to eighteen, were listening to a male speaker. He said that he would rather see his daughter dead than have her virtue violated. Being a child, I didn't exactly understand how one's virtue was violated, but it really scared me that a Mormon father would, under any circumstances, wish his daughter dead. I determined to get as far away from this warped thinking as I could.

Mormonism is a patriarchal religion. The only stature a woman can achieve in the afterlife is in one of the degrees of heaven, and that through the man to whom she is "sealed" in the Mormon temple. So there are no "potholes" for a woman (or girl child such as I was) in Mormonism—just one huge chasm larger than the Grand Canyon.

As an aside, I find it amazing that there is a group of "ex" Mormons who want to retain the "culture" of this religion. To me, that culture is riddled with rules and laws controlling behavior. And a person doesn't need Mormonism to tell her or him that it is a good idea to eat with one's family. So what culture, exactly, is it that they find worth preserving?

In any case, I was very quiet about my beliefs until I "escaped" to college at age seventeen. Even then my family gradually learned of my real thinking as they discovered during vacations my lack of religious practice and lack of desire to raise my children in their church. When I turned twenty-one, I started my search for a bishop with the nerve to excommunicate me. I achieved that at age twenty-three. And once my father died, I simply told everyone the truth. No one since has bothered me about my personal philosophy. That is, except one niece who is determined to have me re-baptized after my death. (Yes, they do that in the Mormon religion—baptize the dead.) And then, a month or so after I wrote the majority of this text, my sister asked me to please stay away from her son so my "anti-god" beliefs wouldn't affect him. She used much stronger words after that, and this made me realize that I had been tolerated but not accepted. My lack of faith amazes, disappoints, and hurts my family and former friends. And few of them are even interested in knowing my philosophy of life.

However, having been an atheist so long, I never felt the need for any validation of my views. I therefore spent my adult years simply working and raising my children. And for my friends and my colleagues at work, religious belief or lack thereof was never an issue. No one ever asked, and I can't remember a conversation even bordering on religion. (Politics is another story.)

This means that my "path" to humanism, such as it was, didn't start until I retired and wanted to find a like-minded community. Before then, while I had read philosophy and studied comparative religions—building my worldview from "scratch"—I hadn't encountered humanism. I found the American Humanist Association online and very much appreciated its resources and community. I have since read the Humanist Manifestos as well as other humanist writings and value the humanist ideal that reason and thought should dominate life's decisions. I also believe my life is consistent with the principles contained in these documents. But I am and have been on my own path.

The counsel to live and let live is for me the most distinguishing feature of humanism. It isn't necessary to "convert" others to one's way of thinking. My life has been sufficiently complicated without making my lack of belief an issue in my home, school, or workplace. So I chart my own course, determine my own virtues, and let others do the same.

Nonetheless, others growing up in a situation similar to mine may find it more difficult to silently suffer an imposed faith. They may yearn to speak out. My suggestion to them would be to do what they find best, whatever that might be: silence, rebellion, or something between.

So I can live and let live even with those who find reasons to do otherwise.

❖

Raúl **Martínez**

Raúl Martínez has a BA in marketing and currently works in IT Project Management. He is the author of the children's book There Is a Purple Dragon in My Washing Machine *which introduces children to the arbitrary nature of belief and the advantages of rational thought.*

In 2014 he became president of the Humanists and Atheists of Las Vegas. He has also previously served as a member of the AHA board of directors.

I

t was my dad who initially set me on my path to humanism. He is an engineer and always has been scientifically minded and a very logical thinker. In the 1970s his heroes were Carl Sagan and Isaac Asimov. He had a subscription to the *Skeptical Inquirer* and would tell me about some of the experiments they did. That is how I learned about challenging astrologers, psychics, palm readers, and other tricksters. It was fascinating to realize that one could scientifically prove that a hoax is a hoax. It was through this publication that my dad eventually came upon Humanist Manifesto II.

My family was Catholic and I was baptized. Although my parents were married in the church, we were not very religious and didn't go on Sundays—not even on Christmas. My grandparents would go to church every Sunday, and I went with them once or twice. But I found it boring and stopped. We didn't have any crosses or pictures of saints in our home. We also didn't have any candles or "shrines," since my mom thought they were tacky.

My grandmother on my mom's side lived with us, and in a drawer she always kept a little bottle of holy water. She only took it out when my sister and I were fighting. She would spray us with it while she ordered us to stop. It was a simple gesture and would make my sister and me laugh—so I guess it served its purpose!

When I was about nine and my sister seven, Catholic guilt got to my mom, and she suddenly felt she was failing when it came to her children's religious education. So she decided, for the first time, to take the two of us to Sunday school.

The teacher there started explaining who God was and what he did. When she was done, she asked if we had any questions. I was the only one who raised his hand. An earthquake had just hit somewhere, and I remembered my parents talking about it, so I asked the teacher, "If God is so powerful and loves us so much, why did he make an earthquake kill so many people?" Her response was that God did not make the earthquake happen; it is just how things occur in nature. So I slowly raised my hand again and asked, "If God didn't make the earthquake, couldn't he have stopped it?" It made perfect sense to me. If everything we knew about God was true, why wouldn't he help us? Why wouldn't he stop humans from suffering? Needless to say, the teacher wasn't happy with my questions!

After it was all over, when my mom picked us up, my sister ratted me out. "Raul got in trouble!"

"Why?" asked my mom.

"Because he was asking too many questions."

"What kind of questions?"

When I told my mom what they were, she said, "Those are very good questions, son."

My sister and I never had to go to Sunday school again.

When I was a young person I didn't have many opportunities to "come out" as nonreligious. But I remember one episode when I was in eighth grade. My school had organized an event on a Friday where at noon they would take us to a nearby Catholic church. Our mothers were invited to join us for a mass in honor of Mother's Day. Since my mother worked as a teacher at another school, she couldn't come. I lived very close to the church so, after mass, I was going to walk home. While in the bus from the school I started to think: *Why do I have to do this?*

When we all got off the bus, I said to my teacher, "My mom is not coming. I am just going to walk home when this is over—and I don't believe in God. Can I go home now?"

My teacher hesitated for a moment and then denied my request. She told me to stay in the back of the church and leave when mass was over. I remember being really angry at the whole situation, which I found completely illogical and unreasonable. To show that I wasn't happy about being forced to be there, I did sit in the back but not in a pew. I sat on the floor. I guess maybe I was hoping for my teacher to look at me, reconsider, and eventually let me go. If not, I was at least content with staging my sit-down protest.

My friends in the back pew were curious. "Why are you sitting on the floor?"

"I don't believe in God," I replied, loud enough for my teacher to hear.

Most of my friends didn't care. They took one glance at me and turned back to listen to the priest. But there was one guy, Fernando, who wouldn't leave me alone. He decided to periodically turn around and mock me in various ways.

During a Catholic mass, the priest will at one point invite everyone to shake hands. It's a symbol of peace and unity in which you turn to the people around you, strangers or not, and shake their hand as you say, "Peace be with you." When the time came to do this, most of my friends in the back row walked over to where I was to shake my hand. I shook their hands, of course. But when Fernando, with a stupid smirk on his face, walked over and extended his hand, I refused to shake it. He got very angry and stretched it out again, saying very forcefully, "Shake my hand." I again refused. So while I was sitting on the floor he kicked me.

From my various life experiences I have concluded that we should be proud of the choices we make. Things do get better.

And while I haven't converted anyone to my viewpoint, I would like to think that I have helped make it easier for others to be less afraid of acknowledging their nonreligious views to others.

When I told my dad that I didn't believe in a god, he said, "Good. Now you know what you are not; the next thing you need to figure out is what you are." When he showed me Humanist Manifesto II, I was "hooked."

❖

James **Nguyen**

James Nguyen is Australian-born of Vietnamese descent, lives in Chicago, and works as a high frequency trader using algorithms, high speed computers, and software to make stock-trading decisions.

At the highest level, what put me on my path to humanism was the need to understand my place in the universe. I think I have always felt the need to have a framework with which I could measure my life and determine its meaning and purpose.

Growing up in Sydney, Australia, there was some amount of religious influence in society, in school, TV programs, and elsewhere. My parents were not very religious in our daily lives. We never went to church or temple, and there wasn't a significant religious undertone to our upbringing. My father, however, is Buddhist, and he would encourage us to pray in that tradition from time to time. Notwithstanding, we didn't get in trouble whenever we didn't pray, nor did he press us when we told him we didn't believe in the supernatural aspects of the religion as we grew up.

As noted, there were some Buddhist aspects in our upbringing that I ended up discontinuing, such as the supernatural elements of prayer, karma, reincarnation, and meditation. The most accurate thing to say is that I have left behind the supernatural reasons for many religious traditions but still continue many of the traditions for other reasons.

I think that there are many secular benefits from continuing some of these practices. For instance, no one can doubt the benefits to mental clarity, stress reduction, and self-awareness that come from becoming increasingly astute in meditation. There is no need to believe in supernatural beings to understand the benefits of being in control of your thoughts, emotions, and other elements of your mind.

A secular benefit of prayer could be the daily reminder of what is important to you and reminding yourself of the dreams and goals that you have for yourself. And if it encourages you to believe in your own ability to achieve these goals, it sounds worthwhile to me to explore how we can provide this benefit in a secular form. Another reason why I continue many traditions, such as Christmas (even though I was never a Christian) is that they are great occasions where family and friends get together and appreciate time with each other, get to know each other, and grow together.

With regard to "potholes" in the traditions of my previous religious experiences, there were many! The main one for me was trying to reconcile the existence of the tens of thousands of different religions in human history. While thinking about this problem, I came across the idea that the human mind is fallible in many ways, among which is the tendency to believe in what feels good and in ideas that are not challenging to our identity.

The more I thought about this and talked with others, I could see how religious ideas may have started and persisted for so long. I understood that what I believe today must be highly correlated with my parents' beliefs. Being in their care for over two decades, I know that their beliefs must be a significant part of my identity, but this in itself is not confirmation of truth. If something is truthful, it should be able to withstand skeptical scrutiny. And so I put my parents' as well as all others' teachings through my own lens of scrutiny, and although many traditions and values stayed the same, the supernatural ones fell away. The values that stayed make a lot of sense to me and fit in well with what humanism represents.

Did I have a "Road to Damascus" experience? My experience was more transitional in the sense that I think I was always a humanist but didn't know I could identify myself as a humanist until I was made aware of the term by my fiancé. It was, however, an extremely euphoric experience when I was made aware of this movement for two main reasons: (1) realizing that I was not the only one with these thoughts and (2) knowing that there were many before me who have philosophized and written about humanist ideas that could help me further form my identity and my ideas.

My family is basically secular in their belief system, so it didn't even come up as something out of the ordinary when I told them about my humanist beliefs. In fact, most agreed that humanism was the most logical life philosophy. They were definitely happy that I had, for the first time, a framework which I could use to guide my direction in life. The response from friends also was good. Since my regular group of friends contains humanists and progressive Christians, no issues have ever come up.

I have spoken to some colleagues about humanism in passing but never in much detail and, again, there were no issues there. Of course, I am selective about which colleagues I discuss this with and haven't yet picked someone who would patently disagree with the ideas. I have usually discussed it if I feel like someone would benefit from knowing that humanism as a movement and collection of ideas exists.

Thinking about the initial period when I first came across the idea of humanism, I was eager to get as much information about it as possible. Most importantly, I wanted to know how humanism, logic, reason, and evidence could provide me with meaning, life purpose, and a framework from which I could understand my place in the universe. One of the most exciting things was realizing that there is enough wonder, hope, majesty, and love in the natural world that life and purpose were possible outside of religion.

Every person starts at a different point in life, from a different upbringing and experience. So my suggestion is this: I would encourage you to continue your natural desire to spend time thinking, researching, and asking questions about life, meaning, how we got here, how to live a fulfilled life, and so on. There is a ton of information available on the Internet, speakers who provide many insights about humanism—which is really the path to living a fulfilled life. And to trust that there are very satisfactory answers to all of these questions that once were thought to only be answerable through religion.

Did I find that my position impacted others to consider making a similar move as mine? Not so much. However, I do invest in the American Humanist Association and the Secular Student Alliance and hope my support helps make the path to humanism easier for current and future generations.

To me, being a humanist means being invested in the future of humanity and other lifeforms on Earth and in the universe. It is a philosophy, a worldview, and a lifestance which holds that:

- We can and must rely on ourselves, each other, and humanity to pave a path for ourselves into the future.

- We don't need, nor should we expect, gods to help us do this. We only have one life that we know for certain and this necessitates that every single moment that passes is a moment that we will not get back. We should appreciate and meditate about this fact.

- We should work hard to ensure that all lifeforms get the chance to live a full life. The idea of heaven is a cowardly notion that lazy people use to avoid facing the reality of life.

I further believe that:

- In the deepest way possible, we are connected with each other and should strive for a reality that reflects this.

- The story of how I, we, all of us came into being is so much more wonderful than any other story told by religion. We are all made of star stuff!

- Religion, on the other hand, to me means dogma, and given that we cannot be so arrogant to think we know everything, this is a patently wrong position to hold. We only have the "best of our knowledge" which is growing all the time.

- I don't think that atheism, per se, is a positive position. Not believing in supernatural beings is not an inspiring position to hold. For me, humanism distinguishes itself from all other forms of thinking as I have indicated.

- Humanism is our best chance of not only survival but also happiness and fulfillment as a species. Honest study of facts, evidence, and data, and reliance on logic and reason are our best attacks against the urges of the reptilian part of our brain.

- Humanism is happiness, fulfillment, fullness of life, love, relationships, being safe at your own home as well as others', continually striving to understand ourselves, each other, and the universe, traveling to the stars—and so many more things!

Lastly, I came across the American Humanist Association in my search for humanism on Google. Being able to search for humanism was a huge step in getting me to where I am today. I believe the AHA is an important piece in breaking down existing barriers in law and government caused by prior religious traditions. It is our voice at the government and legal levels and is pursuing this important—and difficult—task.

❖

Vivek **Palavali**

Vivekanand Palavali, MD, is a brain surgeon by profession, an Epicurean in philosophy, and a documentary filmmaker by passion. Born in India, he migrated to the United States in 1986, became a US citizen, and has been practicing neurosurgery since 1995 in Flint, Michigan.

I was born in South India into a family with a Hindu mother and a father who was born Hindu but became an atheist as an adult. As a young boy I remember believing in the Hindu myths and practicing the rituals. But when I was fifteen years old I became an atheist—not because of my father but because I was exposed for the first time to the theory of evolution, the structure of the atom, and the big bang theory of the origin of the universe. That exciting new knowledge shattered my indoctrination.

But there were some "spiritual" questions that still required answers: Is there life after death? What exactly are subjective, personal, divine mystical experiences? What is the meaning of life? Is there a purpose to my being born? The next few years of my intellectual and philosophical journey, which included going to medical school and becoming a neurosurgeon, answered all those questions. But first I had to deal with and get over the excruciating fear of my own mortality.

It was in my sixteenth year that I was suddenly overcome by haunting thoughts of inescapable death. Unless I had company or distractions, I was left alone with my own terrified mind. The awareness of the finality of death, that existential predicament unique to humans, made me hope for eternal afterlife. But with a skeptical mind and the scientific knowledge I had at the time, I became convinced that no such thing existed. A major source of liberation from that fear was my reading a short story, "The Law of Life," from Jack London's *Children of the Frost* (1902) about his adventures during the Yukon Territory gold rush. I came to realize that the law of life is death, which must be faced boldly and accepted.

A year later, I started medical school, which helped me understand the mechanics of the various organ systems down to the molecular level. I saw these organs, not only when functioning smoothly, but when they deteriorated and failed. With that knowledge birth, growth, and death—incredible as they may be—were mysteries no more.

During my neurosurgery residency, studying the human brain made me profoundly appreciate what makes us human. The 1,500 grams of pinkish-yellow tissue that we call the brain, made up of 100 billion neurons, functions as the central processor of the body. This is what produces our personalities, thoughts, feelings, and emotions that manifest as our actions. Our imagination, creativity, aspirations, and even our ideas about God, purpose, and meaning in life are all the byproduct and reflection of our brains.

This soon made me realize that mystical experience, which was attributed to and thought to be evidence for an external divine being, is nothing but an altered physiology of our brains. Suddenly all the pieces of the puzzle fell into place. Modern neuroscientific knowledge substantiated my understanding that God, the soul, an afterlife, and heaven are all personal, flexible, and ever-changing imaginations that exist internally in the minds of wishful believers who have an emotional need for hope, solace, and comfort.

From that point I became a follower of Epicurean philosophy. Epicurus (341-270 BCE) believed that life is nothing but "particularly fine atoms coming together to form a body and a mind in the form of a single entity, a human being, whose eventual dispersal is inevitable" and that "this dispersal is not to be feared. Such a dissolution of the human being means that the entities that we are cease to exist when we die. Nor is there anyone to whom those terrors, that so many religions threaten people with after their deaths, can happen." He also proclaimed, "Death is nothing to us," and said that anyone who genuinely grasps that truth is liberated from fear of death. He aimed at the good life and happiness in this world. His goal and meaning of life stood for pursuit of happiness—but in moderation. Consequently, I now firmly believe that "A multitude of simple pleasures constitutes happiness." Our days are filled with many simple sources of happiness and acts of kindness, joy, and awe. My subscription to such a secular philosophy actually liberates me from the shackles of religious dogma and gives me a healthy sense of urgency to fully relish this fragile one and only life. My experiences as a neurosurgeon that profoundly altered my philosophy of life, made me an Epicurean, and guide my daily thoughts and actions eventually ended up in a book titled *A Mindful Life: A Brain Surgeon's Personal Experiences and Philosophical Reflections on Living Life Fully.*

As far as the question if there is a purpose to my being born, the answer is, no. I quote Dr. Abraham Kovoor, a rationalist from India: "I am an accidental byproduct of momentary biological activity of my parents on which I neither had choice nor control." My father agreed with that statement and did say that if there had been family planning in the village around the time of my birth, he would have stopped having children after my three older sisters and a brother. I am glad that there was no family planning then but am quite aware and accepting of the accidentality of my birth as well as the possibility that I might not have been born at all. There is no grand plan behind my birth. I was born and I will die. What I do in between those events and how I do it is my meaning of life and the purpose I create for my life. I am responsible for my own actions. I have to take the blame for my mistakes and some credit for my achievements. I have had this outlook since completing my neurosurgery residency in 1995 at the University of Chicago.

After I started practicing medicine in Flint, Michigan (Michael Moore country), I began to develop a passion for documentary filmmaking. Television images of thousands of innocent children and their families being killed frustrated and angered me. Communities were being bombed to dust because of incessant global wars fought for power or "real estate," as Donald Rumsfeld put it—wars fueled by religious fanaticism. As a man of peace, I wanted to do something about it. So I began to write a book about how humans are killing one another in the name of a god that exists only in our minds as a creation of our brains. Halfway through, I realized that my thoughts would make for an interesting documentary instead. And I knew where to start. Ten miles from my hometown in India, on a small hill, is a temple where to this day believers sacrifice chickens, sheep, goats, calves, and buffaloes by beheading them in front of a stone statue goddess who loves animal blood—a startling and sickening image that I had to document. So I bought a high-definition camera, learned how to use it, went to eight countries, did my own cinematography, and produced in 2008 *Creator of God: A Brain Surgeon's Story*.

That film was followed in 2013 by my healthcare documentary, *Bitter Pill: America and Healthcare in America; a Brain Surgeon's Dissection and Prescription*. During one-and-a-half decades of my neurosurgical practice, I was perplexed by how the greedy "medical-industrial complex" is depriving millions of citizens in the most powerful and one of the wealthiest nations in the world of basic quality healthcare. The negative reaction generated in the country by Obamacare, which is trying to bring healthcare to all Americans, first shocked me, then inspired me to comprehensively analyze the complicated, profit-oriented healthcare delivery system in the United States. I am happy to say that the resulting documentary garnered two Michigan Emmy nominations.

In sum, besides being able to help my patients as a neurosurgeon, I am able to pursue my passion of philosophical activism for secular humanism through documentary filmmaking. My basic humanist conviction is to be a good human being and live an enjoyable as well as fulfilling life, with the view that all people come from one source and are deeply and truly connected. We have the DNA to prove it. When I open skulls during brain surgery, I can not tell any difference between the brains of patients of different races, religious beliefs or nationalities, whether straight or gay. And this profound realization of the oneness of humanity is the culmination of my evolution from a Hindu to a humanist.

❖

Steven **Pinker**

Dr. Pinker is the Johnstone Family Professor of Psychology at Harvard University and the author of How the Mind Works, The Blank Slate, *and* The Better Angels of Our Nature. *In 2006 he was honored as Humanist of the Year by the American Humanist Association.*

Two epiphanies set me on my path to humanism. One was a gradual development in my professional life as a cognitive scientist. My conviction that the mind is a product of the brain, that the brain is a product of evolution, and that moral systems must be informed by a scientific mindset, led me to question the common belief that religion is a major source of morality. The other was sudden: coming across the many passages from the Old Testament in which God commands his people to commit rape and genocide.

Nonetheless, I maintain an affection for the traditions of Judaism that I grew up with, and still follow one or two selectively. The traditions were those of Reform Judaism, so they were far from onerous in the first place. At the same time, I enjoy being able to take back the two evenings and days of the High Holidays rather than spending them in a temple. The services have moments of beauty, but virtually the entire liturgy consists of groveling to an egotistical God who is insatiable for flattery, and it began to grate on my nerves.

"How did my family, friends, and colleagues react when I told them about my path to humanism?" I never did tell them because I never thought there was anything to tell. My parents and sister are slightly more observant than I am, and while they don't identify themselves as "humanists," their beliefs are probably indistinguishable from mine. My brother is even cooler toward religion, so there was no problem at all there.

Being a humanist doesn't require hostility toward the beliefs and practices of others. It simply means basing morality and meaning on reason and science rather than on religion, faith, revelation, tradition, or dogma. Although I always have had a vague sense that a scientific understanding of human nature was compatible with a robust secular morality, it was only through the intellectual influence of the philosopher and novelist Rebecca Newberger Goldstein (to whom I am married) that I understood the logic connecting them. (Rebecca, by the way, was recognized as Humanist of the Year in 2011 by the American Humanist Association.) She explained to me how morality can be grounded in rationality, and how secular humanism is just a modern term for the worldview that grew out of the Age of Reason and the Enlightenment (in particular, she asserts, from the ideas of Baruch Spinoza). As I noted in my book, *The Better Angels of Our Nature*, to the extent that the decline of violence has been driven by ideas, it is this set of ideas, which I call Enlightenment humanism, that has driven it.

This seems like a good opportunity to share some ideas I have written or spoken about over the past few years which are relevant to my path to humanism. They are:

- Morality is not a set of arbitrary regulations dictated by a vengeful deity and written down in a book, nor is it the custom of a particular culture or tribe. It is a consequence of the interchangeability of perspectives and the opportunity the world provides for positive-sum games.

- Morality is not just any old topic in psychology but close to our conception of the meaning of life. Moral goodness is what gives each of us the sense that we are worthy human beings.

- It was natural to think that living things must be the handiwork of a designer. But it was also natural to think that the sun went around the Earth. Overcoming naïve impressions to figure out how things really work is one of humanity's highest callings.

- The doctrine of the sacredness of the soul sounds vaguely uplifting but in fact is highly malignant. It discounts life on earth as just a temporary phase that people pass through— indeed, an infinitesimal fraction of their existence. The gradual replacement of *lives* for *souls* as the locus of moral value was helped along by the ascendency of skepticism and reason.

- The indispensability of reason does not imply that individual people are always rational or are unswayed by passion and illusion. It only means that people are *capable* of reason, and that a community of people that chooses to perfect this faculty and to exercise it openly and fairly can collectively think their way to sounder conclusions in the long run. As Abraham Lincoln observed, "You can fool all of the people some of the time and some of the people all of the time, but you cannot fool all of the people all of the time."

❖

Anthony **Pinn**

Anthony B. Pinn, PhD is Agnes Cullen Arnold Professor of Humanities, professor of religious studies, and director of the Center for Engaged Research and Collaborative Learning at Rice University. He is also director of research for the Institute for Humanist Studies.

U

was raised in a profoundly religious environment in Buffalo, New York. With my devout mother providing the biggest and earliest influence and the local minister tapping me for a career in the church, I became "a rising star" in my local African Methodist Episcopal church.

Preaching my first sermon as a preteen and becoming ordained in an evangelical ministry by eighteen, humanism wasn't an available option. In fact, my religion was a speaking-in-tongues kind of faith where one was expected to be regularly moved in a God-fearing way by direct connection to the Holy Spirit.

This faith seemed more than intact as I passed my time in the white fundamentalist West Seneca Christian School and then began college at Columbia University. While in New York, I spent time ministering at Bridge Street AME Church, the influential and oldest continuing African-American congregation in Brooklyn. With Christian faith permeating much of my life and me on the doorstep of a life of notoriety in the church, it was almost impossible to walk down the roads that lead to atheism and humanism.

However, an intellectual inquisitiveness combined with New York City and Columbia University's atmosphere of skeptical exploration was a combination that opened doors to knowledge that conflicted with the Christian story. These also suggested the possibility of better answers to the social problems with which communities grapple than those religion provided. On discovering historical and philosophical truths that didn't fit with a biblical view, I found myself beginning to modify my faith gradually away from the literal Bible and the evangelical position of revealed truth. Over time, the worlds of academia and the church seemed less and less compatible.

It was with such seeds of doubt firmly planted that I went to Harvard Divinity School where they blossomed into a more and more pragmatic approach that embraced realism. Harvard was a place where the Bible didn't take precedence over science and reason. At the same time, I came to better appreciate the pluralism within African American faith communities and saw value in remaining a part of that world. So I continued to adjust my own faith to fit with what I learned about life in and out of academic circles. I was still preaching, but instead of seeking magical unison with the Holy Spirit, I focused on imparting what I learned about ethics and morality.

Even a liberalized belief, however, wasn't going to survive my probing analysis of theism. As I completed the Masters of Divinity program at Harvard and went on to the PhD program there, I realized that the more I asked myself where I could find God's presence affecting the world, the more it became clear that such an effect simply wasn't there. I finally concluded, as I have explained in my book, *Writing God's Obituary*, that "God never existed but has always been nothing more than a symbol, a piece of language and culture constructed by humans."

Many atheists and agnostics I have met, and who have come from religious backgrounds, went through—and may still be going through—a period of anger at the religious mentality. The religious mentality all too often maintains a rigid attachment to a belief system that is not based on evidence and which is willing to indoctrinate others on this extremely weak basis. But that conclusion was such a natural next step in the steady progression of my views that it was accompanied by neither a jarring change nor a period of anger over having been misled. I did not feel lost as a consequence of this decision and did not feel like I'd lost anything substantive.

Having earned my PhD at Harvard in 1994, I went on to teach first at Macalester College in Saint Paul, Minnesota. My atheism wasn't a secret, and my research and dissertation helped me explore how and why humanism is an important aspect of African-American thought. When my dissertation was published as a book, it first provided a focal point for having this conversation in broader academic circles. But the conversation suddenly became widespread when the *Minneapolis Star Tribune* ran a story on my arguments and highlighted my atheism.

The article generated numerous letters and calls condemning my lack of belief in God and suggesting that, as an atheist, I shouldn't be allowed to teach in the religious studies department. Such criticisms revealed the prejudice against people who don't happen to believe in a god—since nobody was questioning whether or not professors of one religion could teach about another. Religious parents don't typically have anywhere near the same concern about their children converting from one religion to another, as long as they don't become atheists.

While the college officials stood by me, Minnesotans in and out of the college weren't so supportive. It became apparent that the theistic majority felt free to disrespect the sizable nontheistic minority, but that it was a break in protocol if atheists were to express their honest view of the inadequacies of religion. If anything, this seemed magnified in the African American communities in Minnesota with which I was connected.

Atheists, humanists, and Unitarian Universalists in the Twin Cities reached out to me, inviting me to their meetings and providing a platform to speak. While I had some knowledge of the humanist movement, this was the catalyst that allowed that connection to form. Unfortunately, it also exposed the ignorance and outdated ideas within humanism at that time regarding race issues. But my involvement, and that of others, helped slowly improve that situation as did a gradual move in recent years toward a broader humanist base that attracts younger and more ethnically diverse people. Although there is still a struggle to shed old patterns of thinking, shift movement leadership, and actually do things differently in ways that will help the movement realize its goals of diversity, progress is evident.

Today I continue to teach and am the Agnes Cullen Arnold Professor of Humanities and professor of religious studies at Rice University. In addition, I am director for the Institute for Humanist Studies and a board member of the American Humanist Association. In my work I understand that different theistic traditions have an undeniable and continuing influence and cultural value, making continued study of such a matter of significance.

To conclude, I rejected the concept of God because it has no demonstrated ability to help people based on where they are and in light of the issues with which they wrestle. I view humanism as having that ability as well as the potential to provide for the greater good. So I attempt to bring this perspective to the humanist movement in order to help us embark on our next steps to advancing humanist thought and action.

❖

Harold **Saferstein**

Dr. Harold Saferstein, age eighty-three, is a retired dermatologist living in Arizona. He and his wife Doreen are active in the Humanist Society of Greater Phoenix, both having served as program chairs. He organized and was one of the six lecturers for three courses on humanism for the HSGP, two at local community colleges, and one at the Humanist Community Center. Both he and his wife played a large part in acquiring and renovating the Humanist Community Center in Mesa, and he was involved in establishing a foundation to assure the HSGP's longevity.

have been a skeptic since my high school biology class and became an agnostic in medical school. Then, about fifteen years ago, I became a secular humanist the moment I learned that such a philosophy existed. It occurred when I attended a meeting of the Humanist Society of Greater Phoenix because I wanted to hear the guest speaker, Steve Benson, editorial cartoonist for the *Arizona Republic* and an outspoken freethinker. I joined that day and my wife joined a year later. Today my wife and I have numerous friends in freethought organizations.

Although I was brought up in an Orthodox Jewish family, it was minimally observant. So after my bar mitzvah I didn't attend services again until my first child was born when I was twenty-eight. When I went into practice in Wheeling, West Virginia, my wife and I joined a Conservative synagogue, which eventually merged with a Reform congregation. I was active in the Jewish community there, having served as president of both congregations.

When we moved to Arizona, we joined a Reform temple in Phoenix and resigned about a year after I joined the HSGP. We still consider ourselves Jewish "in spirit" but Judaism, as all religions, depends on faith at the expense of reason. I also find the rituals boring and meaningless and the repetition annoying.

My two younger sons claimed to share my atheism and, although my oldest son is not very observant, he was upset that we abandoned Judaism. Some friends made light of it, most tolerated it, a few became estranged. It really isn't a problem except in one case. A daughter-in-law who is a Reform rabbi insisted we not try to influence her daughter who attends a Jewish day school. I also have several very observant cousins who seem to accept my views—although I'm certain they were unhappy to learn of them. Overall my advice is, don't hide your beliefs from your family and friends. If they cannot accept them, that is their concern.

One close friend became an active humanist under my influence. Although I don't promote humanism aggressively, I try to recruit new HSGP members when someone shows an interest.

It has given me great satisfaction to throw off the yoke of religion. I get gratification out of joining and supporting organizations promoting freethought and reason. Humanism respects reason as the only path to knowledge. Faith, on the other hand, rejects or at least discourages reason.

❖

Herb **Silverman**

Herb Silverman is distinguished professor of mathematics emeritus of the College of Charleston, founding president of the Secular Coalition for America, and a board member of the American Humanist Association. Herb's latest book is Candidate without a Prayer: An Autobiography of a Jewish Atheist in the Bible Belt.

was attracted to humanism as a child, although I had never heard of such a worldview. In the Orthodox Judaism in which I was raised, the performance of *mitzvahs* (good deeds) was encouraged. This seemed like a decent thing to do and made me feel good. But the prayers I recited were a different matter. While they all sounded fine to me in Hebrew, when I began translating them into English and thinking carefully about the meaning of the words, I was often appalled at how the god of the Bible killed or asked us to kill those not like us, and expected our constant praise and worship. I decided to follow only what made sense to me and, at the age of twelve, gave up the idea of God. Thus I became a *mitzvah*-performing atheist, which for me is a reasonable definition of "humanist."

I also gave up the belief that I was one of the "chosen" people—that God had chosen the Jews because he cared more about us and held us to a higher standard than those *goyim* (gentiles). Thus I stopped viewing gentiles as "the other" and established friendships independent of the religion into which they were born. By contrast, I have an Orthodox aunt who for decades has refused to meet my spouse because she is a *shiksa* (female gentile).

The rituals didn't make much sense either, and I eventually stopped doing most of them. For instance, since age eight I had been fasting on Yom Kippur, the holiest day of the year. At fifteen,

I ate. I didn't believe there was a god who would determine on that day (as tradition has it) who shall live and who shall die in the coming year. When an aunt became upset about my not fasting, I pointed out that she also hadn't fasted. Her response was, "Yes, but I didn't have all your education."

I enjoyed studying Torah as a youngster and Talmud was even more fun. The Torah (Hebrew Bible) is the foundation for religious Jews. The Talmud is a collection of writings by rabbinical scholars who attempted to clarify scriptural passages and biblical law. I found it fascinating to read clever commentaries in which different sages made good arguments to justify their points of view even though they came to opposite conclusions. Perhaps such Talmudic study might explain why so many Jews grow up to be lawyers. And atheists. My rabbis encouraged questions, but not "Who created God?" There apparently was no good answer to this decidedly un-Talmudic inquiry.

One rabbi raised the question of why the Torah repeatedly says "God of Abraham, God of Isaac, and God of Jacob," instead of the more concise "God of Abraham, Isaac, and Jacob." His Talmudic explanation was that each of these patriarchs had a slightly different god and that we must all search for and find our own god. I took the rabbi's comment very seriously, and my search at age twelve led me to a god who couldn't possibly exist. I was thrilled by my reasoning, but a little bit frightened. I didn't believe there was a god and I didn't know anyone else who thought as I did. So I was a quiet atheist even before I knew the term "atheist."

That changed as I grew up and, after a while, I wouldn't hesitate to tell people about my views. Religion wasn't much discussed when I lived in New York and Massachusetts, however, but when I moved in 1976 to South Carolina to teach at the College of Charleston, where being an atheist in an academic environment wasn't a problem, the level of discussion increased.

Then I received national publicity in 1990 when I declared for governor of South Carolina, becoming the "candidate without a prayer" in order to challenge the state constitutional provision that prohibited atheists from holding public office. At which point I got a call from a distressed woman in Philadelphia—my mother. I had to agree that the *Philadelphia Inquirer* was not the best way for her to discover that her only child was a candidate for governor—and an atheist. So that was the first political fence I had to mend.

While a candidate I learned about a number of nontheistic organizations, including the American Humanist Association, and said to myself, "That's what I am, a humanist." During that time, whenever I received publicity, I would hear from many others who thought they were the only atheists in South Carolina. Eventually we formed the Secular Humanists of the Lowcountry (an AHA chapter), which celebrates its twenty-second anniversary in September 2016. Even independent-minded humanists enjoy being part of a like-minded community.

When giving talks to local groups, I learned that some were affiliated with the AHA. One speaking invitation came from Margaret Downey, president of the Freethought Society of Greater Philadelphia. She was on the AHA board of directors and asked if she could nominate me for the board. I agreed and was elected in 1998.

I like to think that the AHA promotes my convictions because I played a small part in helping to change AHA convictions. When I first joined the board it contained mostly elderly men (like I am now) who mostly discussed humanist philosophy, how best to define humanism, how humanism differs from atheism, and why the AHA was better than "rival" nontheistic organizations. The AHA has thrived and grown after becoming more activist and cooperative with other organizations.

My advice to others of like mind is to come out of the closet. I regret not having come out sooner. I don't mean becoming an evangelist and going door to door proclaiming the nonexistence of God. But when religion is discussed, as it often is in the South, proudly say what you think. Don't try to convert but answer questions about why humanism makes sense to you. You will likely be pleasantly surprised by how many either share your outlook or become interested in your point of view.

An elevator definition of humanism is "Good without any gods or other supernatural beliefs." The rest is commentary. It includes a commitment to the application of reason, science, and experience to better understand the universe and to solve problems; separation of religion and government; securing justice and fairness in an open, pluralistic, and democratic society; and protecting the Earth for future generations.

Humanists have principles and values, but they are written on paper and not carved in stone. Ethical values are derived from human needs and interests and are tested and refined by experience and evidence. Humanists are guided by the consequences of their actions to individuals, to their families, and to their community. Humanism requires flexibility because the circumstances under which people live continue to change and we discover what works better. I don't spend a lot of time wondering how my way of thinking differs from others (except when I'm in a debate), but I hope to promote humanism by living my life as a humanist.

❖

Sharon **Stanley**

Sharon Stanley is a recently retired New York City special edu-
cation teacher who has also worked as a children's librarian at
her local public library. She and her husband Christopher, who is
an Occupational Therapy Assistant, have been members of the
Ethical Humanist Society of Long Island for 20 years. They
are proud to declare that their son, Gabriel is a first generation
humanist.

As my husband and I were planning our wedding, I was searching for an alternative religion; I was looking for something I could believe in. I had been raised in a Reform Jewish home. My husband was raised in a traditionally Catholic home.

While growing up, I saw many "holes" in the Bible stories and religious beliefs. I especially had difficulty accepting what most Jews believe—that we are the "chosen people." Many Jewish people feel this puts them above all others in God's eyes. I was very uncomfortable with that. I had an extensive Jewish education and went to Sunday school until I was fifteen. As time went by, I came to understand that most people of many religions see themselves as "God's chosen ones."

Equally disturbing was that I saw that religion separates people. It does not lend itself to bringing people together. And historically many wars and hate crimes were the result of religious persecution or intolerance. I began to describe myself as a "religious cynic." Nonetheless, I still clung to the belief that there must be a higher power.

In college I took several comparative religion classes and was surprised to find that all religions had similar stories. Each religion had a "miracle child," "learned" prophets, and a flood story. At that point, my religious outlook began to change and I began to doubt what I had been taught. Although I still clung to the idea that there was a "higher power," I began to think that perhaps since all the religions shared similar stories, they must be referring to the same god but just using different names.

I found myself seeking that higher power and began to follow other paths in an attempt to "feel God." I took classes in astrology, numerology, and crystals. I read books about pagans and mysticism. I learned how to read Tarot cards and even had a "past life regression." My outlook leaned toward the Goddess religions, Native American myths, and other Earth-based religions. At least their ideas of Mother Earth and community made sense to me.

In 1995, I joined the Ethical Humanist Society of Long Island but did not give up my theist beliefs until I went to the American Ethical Union's Summer School Leadership Program in North Carolina in 2004. Previously, I did not even have a clear understanding of what humanism meant. There I met many people from across the movement and began to come to the realization that the reason I have never been able to see or feel God is because he doesn't exist. My experience was very similar to the realization that Julia Sweeney speaks about in her show, *Letting Go of God*: "Oh, my God! There is no God!"

When I was finally able to wrap my brain around the thought that there really is nobody "out there," I came to a place of understanding and peace. At the same time it was exciting because I had to rethink everything I had been brought up to believe. If there is no God, there is no one to condemn. We are all there is. It is our responsibility to make the best of our lives without expecting divine intervention. My commitment to humanism was cemented there and then. My belief in community and caring for the Earth and its people did not change. My thinking continued. If there is no God, what about astrology, magic and ghosts? They must not exist either. There are no jinxes, no superstitions—just people, society, the world. What remains is humanism.

Reactions from my family, friends, and colleagues were mixed. To my surprise, my father fully approved. Apparently he had been an atheist all along. He just went along with what my mother wanted, which was to raise my brother and me as Jews. My friends at the Ethical Society agreed with my new worldview. My colleagues and friends outside of the Ethical Society had mixed opinions. Although they understood our family's commitment to Ethical Humanism, and even admired us for it, no one from our social circle identified as being part of a nontheistic worldview. It became apparent that most would rather join their local church or temple (but not necessarily attend very often) than search for something to believe in. One friend told me, "I know there probably is no God, but I was raised to believe that there is, so I will continue to think like that."

It seems to me that once you say to someone, "I am a humanist," they often react defensively, as if you've made a personal affront to their religion. My intent is not to discuss or deliberate. I do not enjoy debating the existence of a god; it is a waste of time. I do not want to change anyone's thinking nor do I want anyone to change mine. There is a job we all need to do. We still hold the same values. We all want safety for ourselves and our families. That is why I believe that humanism can share a place of comfort among those who practice traditional religions. If we all come from a place of love and reason, we can all focus and help make this world a better place.

Being a humanist means that I get to live out my values every day. Every day I have the opportunity to make the world a better place. I understand that much more can be accomplished with peace, love, and understanding instead of exclusion and conflict. I see miracles in the natural world everywhere I look. And, more importantly, I am aware that we are also humans working together to help each other.

Humanism is very different from most other worldviews. Humanism is inclusive. Most other worldviews and lifestyles are exclusive. Traditional religions leave out personal choice because people see their lives controlled by a higher power. With humanism, we are the responsible ones: people taking care of the problems in the world without looking for someone to save us. It is through social action and ethical relationships that we can right the wrongs. We are in charge. We are responsible. At first this might seem like a scary thought, but it truly becomes empowering. Each of us has the capability to make the world a better place.

I discovered the American Humanist Association as an online presence shortly after embracing atheism. Reading their materials helped reinforce my worldview and helped to solidify and define my beliefs. I embraced the natural world and left my supernatural beliefs behind.

Attending the Reason Rally in Washington DC in 2012, and then again in 2016, creating an annual Darwin Day celebration at my ethical society, and attending conferences and talks involving humanists has helped me to understand that there is much to celebrate in the natural world. There is beauty, awe, and magic in nature, in watching a child learn and grow, and in the arts.

I was inspired by Darwin's ethical dilemma. He was a theist before he began his research and delayed the publication of his historic book because he feared it would destroy religion. Yet, in the end, he did publish the *Origin of Species*. His research was too important to keep silent. Most importantly, his theories negated the belief that different races of humans had different physical and mental abilities. Darwin's theory helped dispel the myths that were at the root of racism.

The American Humanist Association's legal work on behalf of the separation of church and state is on top of my list of important things for which to advocate. Most recently, seeing the American Ethical Union working with the American Humanist Association as members of the Secular Coalition for America makes me realize that both organizations are moving together in the right direction.

A few friends and I have been inspired to start a chapter of the American Humanist Association called "Humanists of Long Island." In barely a year's time, our group has grown from our initial six members to fifteen regular members. In many ways, I believe my life as a humanist activist is just beginning!

❖

Todd **Stiefel**

Todd Stiefel is a secular humanist and a secular activist. He is the chair of Openly Secular and president of the Stiefel Freethought Foundation.

U

For those who are raised in a religious tradition, I believe there is a pattern to how one becomes a humanist. This path is skeptic to agnostic to atheist to humanist. Certainly for me it started with skepticism, a questioning of religious authority and scripture. This was the stage of asking hard questions and receiving soft answers. What followed was a realization that I didn't know if what I was taught was really true. Eventually I found that I didn't believe in gods either. Much later I learned about humanism. I identified with it immediately and realized I had been one for a long time without even knowing it.

I was brought up Catholic, went to Sunday school, had my confirmation, and even went to Catholic high school. I wore a cross around my neck and into my late teens truly believed in God. While I saw the problems with Catholicism early, those problems didn't truly connect for me until I found reason over faith. I learned of the religious-based terrorism in Ireland, the horrors of the Crusades, the debauchery of the popes, and the plague of pedophilia throughout the church. As a result, my experience of becoming a humanist was far more transitional than a sudden shift.

I didn't consider myself a humanist until my thirties, although I was agnostic in late college. The closest thing to a turning point was a course in Old Testament history at Duke University. There is nothing like learning the Bible outside of a church setting to expose reasons for not believing in it. I learned about the pagan myths that were subsumed into the Bible. I found out that my monotheistic religion had a holy book that openly discussed other pagan deities. I learned that my "god" was younger than the Egyptian pyramids and had actually evolved from a polytheistic deity that only gained monotheistic status by agreeing to protect the Israelites in exchange for them stopping worshipping the other gods. It became clear that my religion was as mythological as all other ones.

With regard to how others reacted when I told them about my path to humanism, most were very accepting—although I did lose a couple of friends. I had many surprises from people who unexpectedly told me that they were atheists, agnostics, or humanists as well. While I have definitely experienced some strong discrimination for my humanism, overall it has been very rewarding to be open about my views. I found an enormous community of people who are not afraid to say "I don't know." These are the most accepting and loving people I have ever had the good fortune to know.

There are a number of suggestions I would give others who now follow a path to humanism. First, respect your sense of doubt. That is your internal "bologna detector" telling you that something you believe doesn't make total sense. If you hide from that doubt, it will bring you pain and fear. Your best bet is to ask questions and follow the answers where they lead. You may learn you were wrong about many things and correct about others. That is okay. The search for truth will lead in a circle if you start by assuming you already have the right answers. Challenge your beliefs. Read books and articles. Ask lots of questions and enjoy great conversations. Also be careful to respect other people even if you don't agree with their ideas. While their beliefs may not deserve respect, the people do as individuals. If you decide that religious beliefs are false, remember that you used to hold them yourself. So, rather than showing contempt, show love for those who believe as you used to.

I don't think people consider making a move to become a humanist. Devout theists don't simply decide at a conscious level that they want to stop believing in their deity. You can't decide to disbelieve something that you already believe. I think it is a process that starts at a subconscious level. The mind begins having doubts that are hard to control and reconcile. Many can appease these doubts their whole lives but others find the doubts continually creeping up, even though it would be easier in the short-term if they did not. Eventually, some people can't help but start to think carefully about these doubts at a conscious level. That is the beginning of the path to humanism. It is the conscious questioning and seeking. It is following the path where it leads rather than assuming you are already at the end of the road. Not everyone will continue down the path, but those who follow it to its ultimate conclusion will find they are humanists.

Being a humanist is living life at the intersection of love and reason. It is showing compassion and living a life of integrity. It is also making decisions utilizing freethought, where opinions are formed based on reason rather than authority, tradition, or dogma. Humanism is a way of life where people are in awe of the natural world and flourish in caring interpersonal relationships.

What distinguishes humanism from other ways of thinking? The freethinking piece is different than almost any other form of thought. Religions in particular all require acceptance of either their scripture or their clergy. You must believe in something just because someone or something told you that you must. In humanism, by contrast, you use your own mind to find the truth. Yes, there are some other ways of thought that also reject authority and tradition, but humanism is the only one I can think of that is also grounded in a desire to increase wellbeing for others.

Lastly, I found the American Humanist Association when I did an Internet search for "humanist." The AHA does a great job promoting humanism as a worldview. It is one of my favorite organizations in the secular movement, although we certainly have a long way to go before we dispel all of the myths about people who do not believe in gods.

❖

Derrick **Strobl**

Derrick Strobl is licensed both as a music educator and as an attorney. He has worked in education for over twenty years.

M y life changed after my parents got "saved." Gone were the days of random church attendance at a mainstream, liberal church where I could drink milk and eat cookies in a classroom while my parents listened to sermons about lettuce boycotts. Now my parents had gotten serious about the Bible.

As a five year old, I was proud to host our neighborhood vacation Bible school, bringing friends over for lemonade. We listened to a story from a book made of different colors of construction paper with black for sin, red for blood, white for salvation, and gold for streets in heaven. Near my backyard sand pile, I invited Jesus to live in my five-year-old heart and clean up any terrible sins I might have.

I got more involved in religious activities. At Sunday school I learned songs which I sang with the neighbors while swinging on the swing set. I got a new Bible with pictures and became a champion at memorizing Bible verses.

The church my parents started taking us to was Baptist, where the simple answer to every moral question was "Don't." Don't drink. Don't smoke. Don't cuss. Don't play cards. Don't go to movies. Don't listen to rock music. Don't wear jeans. Don't have long hair. And don't have premarital sex which might lead to dancing.

We each aimed to be more than a "Sunday go-to-meetin' Christian" and tried to be different from what we called "the world."

The world around us was full of liberal Christians "doing away with the Bible and the blood of Jesus Christ" as well as teachers introducing evolution, sex educators, humanists battling to control our minds, feminists and the ERA, communists forcing people to deny Christ, people stopping the violent discipline of children, teens spreading STDs, married couples getting divorced, and allegedly unhappy gay people living in San Francisco. Outside our church, the world seemed like a risky place where Jesus might come back any day.

A number of parents insulated children at private schools and promoted colleges like Cedarville in Ohio and Bob Jones in South Carolina. However, my parents sent me to a public school where I was confronted with challenges to my faith. I told my science teacher that I was not a monkey and stuffed my ears during a school assembly that included rock music. But in spite of the pressure from my church to carry a Bible at school, pray over a school cafeteria lunch, or invite friends to church, uncertainty stopped me.

Witnessing to relatives seemed safer. One asked me what would happen to people who had not heard the story of Jesus. I had assumed that they would all go to hell, but her gentle question stayed in the back of my mind. My grandfather had a science background and had left church as a young person. In answering the question, "What happens when you die?" Grandpa said, "They put you in the ground and you rot." Hoping to encourage me to think of the Bible as literature, my aunt told me she would go to hell to stay warm and read things to me from her Bible that she thought sounded poetic. Later I upset her by changing her stereo channel to a Christian radio station. Eventually I got the opportunity to pressure my aunt to appear to convert while she was in a hospital bed dying from cancer. Yet my aunt's death at a young age showed that life can be painfully short and that prayers can go unanswered. Being told to witness pushed me to consider tough questions related to faith and, as time went on, other experiences brought my faith into doubt.

Being an evangelical Christian complicated my first sexual experience. While part of me was singing "Oh, what a night," I was worried that my dead grandmother might have seen everything from heaven. I went to church the next morning clutching my Bible and promising God that nothing so fun would ever happen again.

While a student at Ohio Wesleyan University, I carefully avoided faith-challenging courses related to the history of the Bible and Christianity. Instead I took what I thought would be a safe class: logic. My atheist philosophy professor showed that when people claim the Bible is true because it says it's true, that is an example of circular reasoning. Years later, his words helped liberate me.

Ironically, the biggest challenges to my faith came when I went to law school in conservative, rural Ohio. At Ohio Northern University I got involved with the student senate and in many issues related to diversity. We helped bring free condoms and HIV testing to campus. Against the advice of many people, we started an alliance to support LGBT students. Groups of Christian students began a petition saying that the town of Ada would be destroyed by fire. A couple of us boldly delivered a package of stones to the Christian group with a note containing Bible quotes about stoning and suggesting that the Christians stone us if they really believed. The controversy got media attention and brought about 200 people to the next student senate meeting. A dean, who was dedicated to nonviolence, organized dialogue opportunities about the alliance. The discussions included anti-gay Christians, loving

Christians, and nonbelievers. Some of the anti-gay Christians admitted that they didn't think women should have the right to vote and they still wanted prohibition to be in place. In trying to prove the anti-gay Christians wrong, I noticed that people eager to put others down have difficulty ignoring what they think they've found in scripture. The discussions also introduced me to the possibility that people could live well beyond faith and left me questioning my own beliefs.

I began exploring other denominations of Christianity and researching other religions. During a recitation of the Nicene Creed at St. Paul's Episcopal Church, I found that I couldn't honestly say the words. So I remained silent. Afterwards I spoke to the rector who explained that the creed need not be said as something literal, that the resurrection of Jesus was not the resuscitation of a corpse, and that the Episcopal Church had a history of making non-literal uses of scripture. When I asked how the process of non-literal interpretation worked, the rector's head dropped in silence. I explored more, but after reading Bishop John Shelby Spong's *Rescuing the Bible from Fundamentalism* and seeing how the Bible had been used as an excuse for many hurtful things, I no longer had reasons to even go on appearing to believe.

Having heard of humanism from sermons against it, I eventually went to the library, looked over my shoulder, and took down a copy of the Humanist Manifestos. I was surprised to see how much I agreed with in those documents. By exploring how I know things and checking the facts, options, consequences, and feelings of people affected by issues, I was using humanist ways of thinking. Humanism fit my support for facts, fairness, and love.

While reading the *Columbus Free Press*, I spotted a listing for the Humanist Community of Central Ohio, a chapter of the American Humanist Association. Until then I had no idea that humanists formed communities where people put reason and compassion into action. I called the number and was greeted by Larry Reyka who asked, "Are you sure you don't want the humane society?" since people often called the wrong number. After asking me what I thought a humanist was, he told me where to come for meetings. I joined the chapter's board and soon became the youngest president of the group, where I continue to organize educational programs and build community.

My experience shows the value of asking questions, having discussions, and letting others know that humanists are organized. As my doubts about supernatural religion became clear, my mother asked "What do you believe?" For me, humanism involves living wisely by human effort and intelligence. There is a lot I don't know, but I do know that we have lives to live, a world to enjoy, and people to share those with. If we use our heads and treat others well, this world and its people may reward us.

❖

Carol **Wintermute**

Carol Wintermute received a Bachelor of Fine Arts degree from Denison University in Ohio and did postgraduate work in psychology at the University of Minnesota in Family Social Science. She was an instructor in that department before becoming education director at the First Unitarian Society of Minneapolis. She also has served as executive director of the International Association of Humanist Educators, Counselors and Leaders, was president of the Humanist Institute, and is now co-dean of the Institute.

𝓤

My father was a fallen-away Methodist while my mother was a devout Roman Catholic. When they married in Philadelphia they compromised and became Quakers, joining the Hicksite sect, the liberal branch of this faith, which was lay led. The Bible was secondary to the Hicksites, who were more interested in cultivating the "light within" than belief in salvation by Jesus. After I was born my family moved to Hartford, Connecticut, and joined a similar group at Yale University. But I was extremely bored by these meetings; we would sit for hours in silence until the "light within" moved someone to say something.

When we moved away from that group, my life became one of wandering into various religious halls with my neighborhood friends as guides. My sister and I even developed a rating system: Catholics, best costumes; Lutherans, best Bible pictures; Methodists, most ferocious and scary; Jews, most sad and serious. At one point I went to a local community church because they had a great ballroom dancing course, with cute boys to boot. I almost agreed to be confirmed, but my parents gently questioned my motivations, and I realized it was the dancing and not the religion that attracted me.

By age eleven I was finished with this odyssey and became an atheist. This wasn't an easy road for a teenager. I was constantly pressed into answering why I was not affiliated with a religious organization. With my parent's support, I stuck to my guns and always argued for my right to be a nonbeliever who deserved the same respect that religious people expected. While I may never have turned anyone into a humanist, I at least was out there. Many came to me to confess their doubts, and I counseled them to remain true to those doubts and seek a truth that seemed reasonable.

In college I heard about Unitarians. When I married Hank Wintermute and had children, we headed for the nearest Unitarian church for what we hoped would provide a comparative religious education for my children and serve our family as a like-minded community. I wasn't disappointed as the humanist congregation we found in Birmingham, Michigan, was a great fit for us. I even became a Sunday school teacher. After moving to Minnesota I took on the responsibility for directing the child and adult education programs at the First Unitarian Society of Minneapolis. I wrote a humanist curriculum that covers early childhood through the adult years. This program takes children and families through developmental stages while addressing issues that pertain to the self, others, community, world resources, and global responsibilities.

At one point I considered getting an MDiv degree. My mother and father were horrified at the idea. Our whole family was nonbelieving and proud of the tradition we had developed on our journey away from Christianity toward humanism. Being a minister, even of a humanist church, was too close to sliding back into the fold.

So, instead, I began taking courses toward a masters and PhD in Family Social Science, which soon developed into a study of moral and ethical development and was quite in line with my humanist philosophy.

Khoren Arisian was the minister at the First Unitarian Society in Minneapolis. Through him I heard of the Humanist Institute, which was being formed in 1982. I was there for the occasion and was invited to be in the first class. After graduating I joined the board of directors, eventually becoming president. I am currently co-dean.

In the late 1980s and early 1990s we moved to Belgium and I became the executive director of the International Association of Humanist Educators, Counselors and Leaders (IAHECL). This was due to Sherwin Wine, president of the Humanist Institute at the time, who was a leader in the International Humanist and Ethical Union, of which IAHECL was the professional branch. I worked from home but loved visiting the humanist centers in Brussels, Antwerp, and Utrecht. I have always hoped to see that model in the United States. These centers were wonderful big buildings that housed classrooms, an auditorium, dining space, meeting rooms, and a publishing house. You could really create humanist community in these places.

I had started Humanist Institute classes before we went to Europe and traveled back for them until I graduated. Meanwhile I made contacts with faculty members at the University of Humanistic Studies in Utrecht. We are still connected with some of the faculty and hope to do future projects together.

It was the Humanist Institute that made it possible for me to meet people from Ethical Culture, the Society for Humanistic Judaism, the American Humanist Association, the Council for Secular Humanism, and so forth. This is because the founders of the Institute began by forming the North American Committee for Humanism (NACH). Without this connection I might never have met people from outside my original Unitarian humanist group. The founders of NACH and the Humanist Institute were real visionaries in bringing all the humanists along the spectrum into meaningful cooperation with one another.

You wouldn't know today, with all our cross pollination, that at one time we spent a lot of our energies telling each other that *our* humanist version was the correct one. Now we are doing great things together and, instead of focusing inward, we are making the world notice that we are here and have something important to say about world issues.

I am proud to be a humanist and associated with people who take responsibility for their contribution to the welfare of the Earth and its inhabitants and are ready to work together to make it good for all.

❖